How to Get Rich Right

The Kingdom Secrets for Acquiring Wealth

John Elliott Churchville

The Virtuous Entrepreneur
An imprint of Churchville Triad Consulting Group

Copyright © 2018 by John Elliott Churchville

All rights reserved. No part of this book shall be reproduced or transmitted in any form or by any means, electronic, mechanical, magnetic, photographic (including photocopying), recoding or by any information storage and retrieval system, without prior written permission of the publisher. No patent liability is assumed with respect to the use of the information contained herein. Although every precaution has been taken in the preparation of this book, the publisher and author assume no responsibility for errors or omissions. Neither is any liability assumed for damages resulting from the use of the information contained herein.

Cover design: Nancy-Ellen Churchville

ISBN-13: 978-1986340830

ISBN-10: 198634083X

BISAC: Business & Economics/Entrepreneurship

Table of Contents

Introduction

Set a S.M.A.R.T. Financial Goal	1
Know, Accept, Believe in, and Love Yourself	3
Join a Master Mind Group	5
The Power of an Idea	7
You Need to Persevere	9
Defining Success	11
Develop an Entrepreneurial Mindset	12
Deciding What You Will Give for What You Want	14
Getting Clear about Your WHY	16
Confronting Your "Who Am I" Question	18
The *Law of Iron Will*	20
Champion a Noble Purpose	22
Concentrate on a Worthy Dream	24
Overcome the Seven Basic Fears	26
Three Core Leadership Values	30
Take Small Deliberate Steps	33
Seven Proven Success Principles	35
The *Law of Speech*	41

Table of Contents

The Threat and Promise of Change	43
Plan Your Estate from a Wealth Perspective	44
The Principle-Centered Leadership Paradigm (PCLP)	51
Build Your Self-Confidence	57
Twelve Components of True Wealth	59
The Moral and Ethical System of *Maat*	61
Ten Spiritual Virtues of *Maat*	66
Seven Spiritual Principles of *Maat*	72
Jesus' A.S.K. Principles	77
Jesus' Teaching on Emotionalizing Your Intention	79
Jesus' Teaching on Kingdom Entrepreneurship	82

Introduction

What do you want in life? Is it money, fame, fortune, magnificent health, happiness? Is it to travel or live in a new home? Whatever you may want in life, you have to start somewhere at some definite point or place. If you're reading this, you're already considering owning a business of your own. That's a great place to start, but it's only the beginning.

You need to have a dream so big, so wonderful, and so far-out that you can't attain it by yourself. The dream must be larger than earning extra money. It must be greater than simply creating an additional income stream for you and your family. It must be huge enough to consume your passion and interest for a lifetime: it must lead you to substantial financial wealth, or it is a waste of your time and energy.

The business you choose to engage in must be compatible with getting you to the dream you have. It cannot be the dream, but it must be able to carry you on the road to your dream. I can assure you that if you read, digest and put into practice the teachings and suggestions in this book, you will be helped to get to the dream that you have for yourself and your family.

This book will not only help you succeed in the business you ultimately choose, but also help you to focus on the dream you have for yourself and provide you with the tools to help you attain it. Consider this book as my personal investment in your future as a productive and important asset to your own company. I am looking for people whom I can groom for success in every area of their lives. Your success matters so much to me, that I'm willing to make a lifetime investment in you—a lifetime of training, coaching, encouragement and even offering you greater business opportunities that will allow you to thrive.

Ultimately, I am in the business of developing successful entrepreneurs who want to grow without any limitations or barriers being placed in their way. Whatever you really want in life, if I choose to be your business coach, you will be part of a family that always supports you in attaining what you want for your life.

John Elliott Churchville
March 23, 2018

Set a S.M.A.R.T. Financial Goal

It's important that you set a Specific, Measurable, Achievable, Realistic and Time-bound (S.M.A.R.T.) financial goal. This process begins the moment you set a specific dollar amount that you intend to earn. Your choice of a very *specific* amount of money that you will earn automatically makes your goal *measurable*—you'll know exactly when you reach your goal. There will be no confusion because you've set your target and will know the moment when you hit it.

The next issue to decide is whether what you have set as a financial goal is *achievable*. This is the tricky part. If you lack self-confidence or doubt your own abilities, then you will not achieve your goal because you have already determined in your own mind that you can't achieve it. So the issue of achievability is an internal problem for you, not an external one that can be imposed on you by others' beliefs or doubts about you. There were lots of people who once thought that having a small portable computer device that could fit in your pocket and be operated without wires or cords was not an achievable goal. They were all wrong—your iPhone or Smartphone proves that! The point is that what is *achievable* for you is what you **BELIEVE** you can achieve. You are the only one who can decide what's *achievable* for you!

Deciding whether the financial goal you set is *realistic* has more to do with timing than with possibility. If you went out in a field and planted wheat today and then went out to that same field tomorrow and tried to harvest wheat, there'd be no wheat to harvest because your expectation was not *realistic*. Why wasn't it *realistic*? It wasn't *realistic* because it ignored the *Law of the Farmer* which says that what you plant today will not grow overnight and be ready to harvest tomorrow. There will always be a time lag between the time you plant something and the time that what you planted is ready to be harvested.

Finally, when you set your definite and very specific financial goal, you must set a definite and specific *time-bound* date by which you intend to reach that goal. This is important because it allows you to adjust your plan for reaching your financial goal if you have either overestimated or underestimated the *time-bound* date it will take to reach your goal.

There is a lesson in all of this that relates to your decision to start your own business. You must take the time to plant before you harvest what you planted. Starting a business requires a period of planting (learning, building relationships with and serving people) before a financial harvest is possible. You cannot afford to have a "get-rich-quick" mentality. You must adhere to the laws of nature and science that teach you that belief in yourself, thorough knowledge of your business, and taking the time to develop positive relationships with people will ultimately bring in the tremendous financial harvest that you want.

Know, Accept, Believe in, and Love Yourself

Each person who has ever become extremely successful in business has had one important and unmistakable trait in common: they each knew, accepted, believed in and loved themselves. Knowing, understanding and loving one's self is the bedrock upon which true wealth, prosperity and personal success are built. But, knowing, understanding and loving one's self can be extremely difficult because there are so many distractions around that most people don't take the time to figure themselves out until much later in their lives. The busyness of life—earning a living, raising a family, coping with the stresses and strains in life—often overwhelms people, so that when they get the chance to assess themselves, they're too physically tired or mentally exhausted to do so.

Because you're on the path to becoming a successful entrepreneur, you must take the time to get to know, understand, accept and love who you really are. You need to make a list of all your strengths—1) those things you do really well; 2) those skills and abilities that you bring to the table; 3) those qualities that showcase your greatest character traits; 4) those qualities that show off your best people skills; and 5) those situations that allow you to do what you enjoy most. Then make a brief mental note about your weaknesses—1) those things you don't do well; 2) those skills and abilities that you can't bring to the table; 3) those qualities that showcase your greatest character flaws; 4) those qualities that expose your worst people skills; and 5) those situations that make you do what you hate. Although you should write down and keep a copy of all your strengths, you should NEVER write down your weaknesses—if you do, they will become worse! Just make a quick mental note of them so that you can avoid situations where they may come into play. (Feed your strengths and starve your weaknesses. Be sure that you NEVER divulge your weaknesses to others—they will always hold them against you!)

Build who you are *now* on the foundation of your strengths. Just as you are no longer a baby in diapers, a 7-year-old playing ball on the sand lot, or a teenager rebelling against your parents, you are *not* who you used to be! You are ever-changing, ever-evolving, and always getting better, smarter, wiser and surer of yourself and the gift that you are to the human race. Learn to encourage yourself, accept yourself and love yourself so that you can encourage, accept and love others.

Love must start with you—know yourself so that you can love yourself and the people with whom you will do business.

Join a Master Mind Group

The history of the Master Mind group can be traced back to multi-billionaire and philanthropist Andrew Carnegie. He associated himself with like-minded people who were innovative, forward-looking and resourceful in their own respective fields. He called this association the Master Mind, based on the truth that when two or more people come together to carry out a definite purpose, then an additional "Mind" comes into play, making the whole group greater than the sum of its parts.

Carnegie's Master Mind group consisted of people such as Henry Ford, Charles Schwab, Alexander Graham Bell, Thomas Edison, and J. P. Morgan, to name a few. Each person found a way to help bring business to the others in a spirit of harmony and non-competition. The result was that each Master Mind group member became exceedingly wealthy.

The secret of Master Mind groups is that the members come together to help one another succeed in whatever business each person may be in. There is no competition allowed in such a group, because only one person or business of a specific type is allowed to be part of that group. So, if you are selling insurance or offering travel services, you would be the only such business person allowed in that group because the Master Mind concept requires each participant to bring something to the group that no other member brings.

In our time, Business Networking International (bni.com) and Le Tip International (LeTip.com) are examples of Master Mind groups. In each case, every member seeks to help the other members by marketing their businesses, and in turn, the other members market that member's business as well.

The benefit of belonging to a Master Mind group cannot be overstated. The first obvious benefit of membership in such a group means that as you help other members of the group to prosper in their businesses by referring people you know and trust to them, they refer people they know and trust to you. Referrals received from people who have trusting relationships with others are much more likely to end in on-going business relationships for you than what you could gain solely on your own.

For example, in a recent year, BNI, a world-wide organization with over 190,000 members, noted that **6.6 million referrals** generated by its members led to **$8.6 billion dollars of business** for BNI members.

Since history has taught me that the Master Mind concept works for anyone who uses it, I urge all serious entrepreneurs to connect with an established Master Mind group, such as the ones mentioned above.

The Power of an Idea

It's amazing how ideas affect all of us. Most of the things and people you like are based on the idea of them you have in your own head. By the same token, most of the things and people you don't like are based on the idea of them in your head. The key ingredient here is that your perception of people, places and things—indeed, your view of the world—is always a creation of your own thinking. That's why how you think and what you think about are so crucial to your success as an entrepreneur.

Successful entrepreneurs are open-minded and relate well to people without branding them good or bad. They have come to understand that people are just like them—sometimes good and other times not so good; sometimes dependable and sometimes not so dependable, and the list goes on.

But what successful entrepreneurs have learned is that they can be good more often than not and dependable more often than not by controlling the thoughts they think and the ideas that they allow to come into their heads. There are many ideas that you can use to control your thinking habits, but there are four powerful ideas which have the power to move you from scarcity to plenty and from surviving to thriving.

The first of these powerful ideas is deliberately deciding to have and keep a positive mental attitude. You can form this habit by mentally willing it to be so and thinking of this idea every day. Instead of complaining about something that looks like a disaster that has confronted you, you can rather look at your situation as an opportunity to learn how to cope with and overcome adversity. This powerful idea, this decision to have and keep a positive mental attitude regardless of your circumstances, will keep you upbeat, grateful and thankful. Without gratitude for life, liberty and the pursuit of happiness, and thankfulness for being alive, you cannot succeed either in business or at living life in general.

The second of these powerful ideas is determining to stay in sound physical health. Physical health has more to do with the content of your thinking than you imagine. Scientists tell us that negative ideas that you persistently think about—worry, anger, resentment, hatred, revenge—lead to physical (and sometimes mental) illness. On the contrary, they tell us that positive ideas that you persistently think about—love, joy, music, appreciation, praise, beauty—lead to the maintenance of physical health. By all means, go to the gym and work out, but don't neglect to work out of your mind the negative ideas that will keep you from living the abundant life of a successful entrepreneur.

The third powerful idea is keeping harmony in your personal relations. One problem that always arises in most human relationships is the belief that one person must be wrong if the other person is right. You have the power to solve this dilemma for yourself quite easily, if you adopt the position that you will commit to listening to people for the sole purpose of understanding them from their point of view. You are not a judge who condemns people who disagree with you. You don't have to agree or disagree with any person. You only need to hear, understand and communicate to that person that you have heard and understood their position.

When you speak to people, you should be trying to communicate as clearly as possible so that they understand you from your point of view. You don't need people to agree or disagree with you. You only need to be sure that people understand what you communicated to them. You should always avoid arguing or debating people with whom you intend to do business. Wait until you're ready to run for political office to do that!

The fourth powerful idea is having a hope of future achievement. This is an extremely powerful idea because it will get you through the disappointments, delays and disasters that happen on the way to your success. As you keep your hope alive that your business will prosper and bring you the financial rewards you deserve, then you can smile when you must deal with disagreeable people and circumstances.

You Need to Persevere

The most difficult growth stage that all truly successful people must face squarely and master is that period of time which inevitably separates the *here and now* uncomfortable place of interminable struggle from the *then and there* elative state that is what you believe to be success. This is the period of time—often long and disappointing—when nothing seems to be happening and you feel stuck in a quagmire that borders on hopelessness.

This is the stage when self-doubt and the doubt of others around you very nearly cause you to give up. Most people who have gained success will not talk much—if at all—about this period of the dark night of the soul.

Everyone who achieves personal success has had to pay their club membership dues in this very difficult, and yet defining place. No one has arrived at the success destination without having collected some scars (and been part of the collateral damage) along the way. So, to expect to be successful without incurring some suffering—whether at the physical, mental, psychological or emotional level—is to expect to build muscle mass without painful daily exercise, play the piano as a virtuoso without perfect practice over long periods of time, or win a world boxing title without having to train relentlessly and take some knock-out hard punches without succumbing to them. In fact, the role of suffering in your life is the discipline that makes you strong and prepares you to manage the wealth that will ultimately be yours.

This is the growth stage where you must use the period of personal suffering as your rehearsal and perfect practice space for behaving as the successful person you aspire to become while in the throes of personal pain. This is the place where, despite the pain of adversity, hardship and extreme difficulty, you begin to take on the behaviors and attitudes associated with living the life you have focused on since the beginning of your quest for success. It is here that you learn that you are, in this pain-filled moment, what you have always determined, aspired and struggled to become. In other words, you have so envisioned yourself from an Entrepreneurial Mindset of success that you are successful long before it is apparent to you or anyone else!

What you will learn in this very tight, uncomfortable place is that success and acclaim are not one and the same. If you are not lauded for the depth and breadth of your accomplishments and the value you have already created for others, then that failure of others to recognize what you have done is completely unrelated to your personal success. You are what you think, believe and behave that you are, regardless of your present circumstances.

Your challenge as an entrepreneur is to live as if the future were in the present, without regard for the physical and visible impediments that currently belie your future status. In order to reach the threshold of the series of events that will catapult you into the manifestation of all that you have worked for, you must manage well the most difficult and discouraging period of deep suffering that comes inevitably at the crossroads of your present situation and your future goal. And it is at this precise moment that you need to learn that perseverance is your best—and oftimes only—friend. Never give in! Never give out! Never give up!

Defining Success

Everyone wants to be successful—whatever that turns out to be. So the first thing that you must do is figure out just what success means to you personally. There is no "one-size-fits-all" here—you must define that elusive thing called *success* for you.

For many people, success is what they see in other people—their external appearance or their high-end lifestyle. The problem with this appearance definition is that you have no real sense of what lies deeper than the surface. What you may be thinking is success is a good front, a public show for your and others' benefit. You see the big house, the new car; you hear about the vacations in Maui and believe these things to be proof of success. What you don't see are the mortgages, the car notes, the credit card debt, the stress, the worry, the hidden maladies and the pressure that these apparently successful people are under to keep up appearances.

So, you cannot take the easy—and deceptive—road that uses what someone else's life looks like on the outside as your personal definition of success. You must do the hard work of asking yourself some tough and penetrating questions and thinking through the answers carefully. It would be a terrible waste of your time and effort to go on a false quest for success, only to find yourself stuck in a miserable situation that brings you no joy or personal satisfaction. So where should you begin?

You must begin your quest for success by understanding the answers to two fundamental questions: "Who am I?" and "What is my purpose in life?" These two questions often require an entire lifetime to answer fully and completely. But the good news is that you don't need full and complete answers to these questions before you begin your quest for whatever you ultimately determine to be success for you.

The great thing about life is that it gives you room to think larger thoughts than the current situation in which you may find yourself. You may be parking cars today, but you could be doing something entirely different tomorrow. However, the issue is not *what* you're doing today or tomorrow. Rather it is how you *think* and *feel* about *what* you're doing today and tomorrow and the *meaning* you attach to your life as a *person* and a *doer*.

Develop an Entrepreneurial Mindset

How you perceive yourself, your life, your family, your work, your relationships—indeed, how you see all of life, the world and your place in it—is based upon your mindset. The power of mindset is so enormous that it is the major determinant of how, and under what circumstances, you will live your life.

Mindset is the way you think, what you think about most and the process you use when you think. More pointedly, in order to be successful in your own business you must adopt a focused Entrepreneurial Mindset—a way of thinking that seeks to maximize your personal development, your highest and best use, the resources you receive, and the resources you create. Such a mindset is the basis for success in business and in life.

In this context, then, you need to develop a dynamic personal philosophy that values your own personal, internal growth and development as the primary by-product of the life you live, the work you do, and the goals you set for yourself. After all, you are the only one who must live with you as long as you live, so your personal growth should matter to you at every age and stage of your life. Such a personal philosophy is dynamic in the sense that it expands and contracts depending on whether you grow or shrink in your thinking and behavior.

This means that you should create mission, vision and values statements that reflect the highest standards of honesty, integrity, fairness, mutual respect and cooperativeness. These same internal values must guide your external dealings with other people. This also means that you must make a commitment to function in the most principled way to put your internal values into external practice.

The purpose for creating a dynamic personal philosophy is to provide yourself with a blueprint, a roadmap, a system that will guide your thinking and behavior to the goals you have set for yourself. A blueprint, roadmap or system is a set of detailed methods, procedures and routines established or formulated to carry out a specific activity, perform a duty, or solve a problem in a routinized, predictable way. Thus, a system is a tested, tried and true program that, if followed, will always yield the result for which it was created. If you use and follow a blueprint for building a house, a roadmap for getting to a specific destination or a sales and marketing system, you will always get the same predictable result—a house built to specifications, a journey completed, a financial goal met.

The dynamic personal philosophy that you create must be effective and efficient so that you can attain maximum personal development as well as the highest and best use of yourself, the resources you receive and the resources you create. This is urgent because you have only one life to live. Accordingly, you should use the finite time you have been allotted wisely. You should always be guided by principles of the Entrepreneurial Mindset: *maximum personal development and highest and best use of yourself, the resources you receive and the resources you create.*

Deciding What You Will Give for What You Want

When you decide to go into business for yourself, you decide that you want to actively control how much money you earn. Once you've made that decision, you must decide what you are willing to give in exchange for your desire to be your own boss.

There are only two commodities that you have to offer people: goods and services. In either case you must give something in order to receive the money you intend to earn.

It should not surprise you that many people in business give the least of themselves in order to gain the most for themselves. But the secret to success and its companion—wealth—is not giving the least, but giving the most. So, just what does giving the most mean?

Giving the most means giving everything you have to the business you choose, regardless of the compensation you receive for your work. This idea is a problem for business people who are not doing well in their chosen field, but it explains what separates the barely surviving from the abundantly thriving business person.

The person who gives little only gets little in return, while the one who gives much receives much in return. It is the *Law of Reciprocity*—what you give comes back to you in the same measure that you gave it except for one big thing. When you give the least in order to be compensated for the most, then you receive much less than you gave. On the other hand, when you give more than what you expect to be compensated for, you receive back much more that is pressed down, shaken together and running over in abundance.

As you think about the goods and/or services that you will be offering people in the business you choose to engage in, remember that you must give the best of yourself to that business in order to succeed, grow and prosper. The days of the mom and pop proprietary business are gone. Today any business you engage in must be programmed to grow larger, develop people who can run it successfully, and provide you the opportunity to hand it off or sell it later at a significant profit.

This means that you should choose the business you intend to own wisely, considering the future of its related industry and the potential growth possibilities it offers. You should also consider what that business brings to the table to make people's lives better. One of the greatest feelings you can have as a successful business person is to know that while you are making profits, the people you are serving through your business are benefitting from the goods or services that you are providing.

As you consider these things, ask for help until you receive it, seek for guidance until you get it, and knock on the door of opportunity until it opens wide to you.

Getting Clear about Your WHY

Many people talk about wanting to own their own business one day. Their reasons go from wanting to be their own boss to living the lifestyle to which they want to become accustomed. But most people who talk about owning their own business one day will never do more than talk about it.

People, who are serious about owning their own business, research different business opportunities, read up on the businesses they have an interest in, and begin the process of deciding which business is most compatible with who they are as people. This work of investigation that they do helps to focus their desire to own a business and to fuel their enthusiasm to find the right business to own.

This is the process that most business owners go through. They use their minds, they get the facts, and then they make a definite decision about which business option they will choose. What many people leave out of the process is an understanding of WHY they go into a specific business in the first place.

It has been estimated that 96% of all businesses started will fail within 10 years. With such an alarming statistic like this around, one wonders why anyone would go into business against such odds. If everyone who started a business believed that she or he had only a 4% chance of success, there would be no new businesses started and the economy would immediately grind to a halt.

However, people are going into business every day, going against the odds that they will probably fail. It would seem that the 4% who succeed in business over the long haul know something that the 96% don't know—they know their WHY and it guides them to prosperity.

When you talk to successful business people, you will find that their WHY is greater than just wanting to make money, or to become a millionaire. If the reason you are planning to go into business is just to make money, you will probably end up in the 96% failure group. Although earning money is important and necessary, it is not enough of a WHY to get you past the 96%.

Your WHY must come from inside you—it must be greater than merely making money. It must be so deeply thought through that it will sustain you in hard times and difficult circumstances. Your WHY must be so strong that it motivates you to get up every day, face the "no's" and other rejections you will face, and yet empower you to get up the next day and the next day after that until your business blossoms, buds and thrives.

Knowing your WHY is so powerful that it will catapult you into success, regardless of the odds against you. So, invest the necessary time in thinking about your WHY and make sure it is large enough to see you through to success.

Confronting Your "Who Am I" Question

The *Law of the Farmer* teaches that what you plant today in a field will not grow today, nor will what you harvest from that field in the future bear any resemblance to what you planted today. The *Law of the Farmer* also teaches that crops take a lot of time to grow. Accordingly, you have to develop the patience to wait for whatever you have planted to grow in its own time—it can't be rushed. It must grow at its own pace. There is no way that you can rush the growth process. In the same way, you must learn to be patient with yourself as you grow the business you intend to own—you will not conquer your bad habits or develop an Entrepreneurial Mindset overnight. But you must start by planting seeds in the ground of your mind—seeds that will yield a harvest that will develop your character as you grow your business.

The *Law of the Farmer* teaches that you cannot begin to plant any seeds until you have prepared the soil to receive them.

The "Who am I?" question is the most important question that you can ask, because the answer to that question describes the soil—your identity (the real YOU)—that must be prepared for any planting that will be done in your life.

When it comes to the values you hold and the behaviors you practice, with some patience and perseverance, you can always find most answers within yourself or within your immediate family. But the "Who am I?" question—the question related to the very essence of your existence—has answers that are external to you. In other words, you cannot look within yourself to discover who you are. Your own internal explorations will yield only your values at best, but will not disclose the compass by which you travel in life. Your notion of your own identity is learned from others outside yourself.

There are many external voices telling you who you are: your family, the schools you attended, your religious institutions and advertising and commercial messages, to name just a few of the myriad voices that scream every day into your ears that you are what they say you are.

So the real challenge is finding the external voice that tells you the whole truth, the objective, unembellished, certain, there's-nothing-in-it-for-the-truth-teller truth. In order to be the voice of truth, this voice must speak based on irrefutable laws of nature—laws which have the same weight as the laws of gravity, physics and mathematics.

Such a voice is found in the *Law of Attraction*. What you focus your mind, your feelings and emotions on is what is drawn to and attracted to you by you. So, one way to find out who you are is to consider carefully and study the people, places and things that come into your life. The old wisdom proverb says, "As a woman thinks, so is she." In other words, at this very moment of your life, you are what you have thought about the most.

However, the great thing about life is that nothing stays the same. The irrefutable *Law of Change* teaches you that you cannot and will not stay where you are. Change will impact you and force you into doing and being more than you are right now. Change will use such events as death or disaster, loss of income or an increase in your family's budget to make you change. Whether you like it or not, you are a person who is undergoing the process of change.

The good news is that you don't have to wait for a death or disaster to hit you in order to make a change. You can be proactive and change yourself! In fact, you're already in the change process—you're looking at starting a business of your own. That's certainly a change from what you were thinking at an earlier stage of your life. The fact that you are changing means that you are a person who is ever changing, ever evolving, and ever moving toward a definite goal—even if that goal is not very clear to you yet.

The *Law of Iron Will*

The key element of preparation for success in your business is your understanding and utilization of the *Law of Iron Will*. The *Law of Iron Will* requires that once you make a decision, you must be unwavering in carrying it out, despite whatever obstacles or apparent impossibilities confront you. You cannot second-guess yourself because other people and/or institutions have issues with what you have decided to accomplish. The *Law of Iron Will* allows you to commit your decisions to God and resolutely carry them out, no matter what the odds of your success may be according to the well-established and revered pundits of the day.

Every truly successful person has had to take a stand on ground that was not confirmed or believed in by others. Every significant breakthrough in science, education and industry has come as the result of single-minded, steadfast opposition to the conventional wisdom of naysayers who oppose change and cling to the presumed safety of the *status quo*.

The key to the *Law of Iron Will* is your definiteness of purpose. By focusing on the definite object that your decision represents and concentrating on that object while waking and sleeping, you develop the toughness of mind, tenacity of spirit and tautness of emotions to withstand, counter and overcome all the objections and negative assaults of the do-nothings and under-achievers who don't have the courage and drive that you do.

The *Law of Iron Will* supports and cradles you during the difficult and oft-times lonely struggle to bring to fruition the new product, service or application that you have created through utilizing your imagination and the concomitant skills and abilities that you have developed along the way.

The *Law of Iron Will* is the full body, mind, spirit and emotions armor that not only protects you in the thick of all aspects of battle, but also allows you to simply stand your ground, unmoved and unshaken by the negative forces arrayed against you.

Finally, you can't continue to think about success in the abstract: you must speak its definition to yourself every day. **"Success is maximizing my personal growth and development, the highest and best use of myself, the resources I receive, and the resources I create, with the intent to become all that God has created me to be."** Thus, success is a competitive activity in which you engage *only* yourself and no other person. You are not in competition with anyone else, because no one is willing to give more than you give, care more than you care, or provide the service you provide above and beyond what you are compensated. You are the only person who can keep you from attaining the success that is uniquely yours. Your success is measurable both in quantitative and qualitative terms by examining your own life in the light of the *Law of Iron Will*.

Champion a Noble Purpose

One of the major keys to personal success is choosing, finding, discovering or otherwise creating a noble cause or purpose that does not benefit you personally. Service to others is a prerequisite to your personal success. Your genuine concern for others, demonstrated by your giving of your time, talent and resources to a worthy endeavor, becomes a catalyst for moving you toward your own destiny.

As you invest the best of yourself in a noble purpose that has no visible strategic relationship to your personal or business goals, you are planting the seeds of your own business success. However, the motivation for your service to others must be pure: you must serve with no expectation of receiving anything in return—no award, reward, recognition, press coverage or opportunity to network with persons whom you believe could forward your personal agenda—not even your desire to hear a simple "Thank you."

Your reward for championing a noble purpose is your willingness to serve others from a God mindset. Such a mindset seeks the best for others with no concern to gain a personal benefit. To serve from a God mindset is to choose to consider the welfare and interests of others over your own welfare and interests to such an extent that you can freely and happily give others your time and resources that you could profitably invest in service to your own agenda. Thus, serving from a God mindset is not being patronizing or condescending to others, but putting others on an equal footing with you. The energy you use to benefit others is at the same level of intensity as that which you use to benefit yourself.

You can only provide this free, no-strings-attached service to others when you realize that you are a child of God who has an unlimited supply of resources to bless others without the possibility of exhausting those resources in a manner that could possibly be detrimental to you.

Many people serve others for the wrong motives and, therefore, serve from a position of weakness. To serve others because you are compelled, either by job title, contract or forced, uncompensated servitude is to serve from a position of weakness. To serve others from a God mindset is to serve from a position of strength. Your service is not coerced, purchased or otherwise performed because you're seeking an advantage, relationship, strategic alliance or other consideration that will inure to your personal benefit later on down the line. Your God mindset service to others originates in and operates from a position of strength—your knowledge of who you are and Whose you are, as well as the inestimable value that your presence and personal involvement brings to others just because of your divine connectedness.

Because championing a noble purpose is directly related to your own personal destiny, you must choose it carefully. You may not be called to support a popular charity or heart-string-pulling charitable endeavor. It may be your lot to serve a noble cause that is not recognized as such by many. Indeed, the noble purpose you end up supporting may be one in which you have no passionate interest.

So, you must consider what your motives are when you choose a noble purpose to embrace and/or support. It is at this point that self-examination, criticism and self-criticism will bring you back to the *Law of Iron Will*.

You cannot know your true motives for doing a thing or choosing a particular path. But you can challenge yourself to examine your motives and seek guidance from above, as well as from others around you. This is true not only with respect to what motivates you to choose a worthy purpose to champion, but also applies to the choices you make in every other area of your life.

Concentrate on a Worthy Dream

One of the signal endowments of human beings is our ability to imagine a situation, circumstance or reality that we have never experienced in the past. It is the gift of seeing the future, as well as the capacity to create what we have seen internally into a visible manifestation that we and others can see externally. Your endowments of imagination and creativity are proof that you have God's DNA within you. It is also evidence that the *Law of Concentration* is immutable.

The *Law of Concentration* teaches that it is the focused attention of your imagination that creates your future. It is your disciplined thought life that is the major determinate of your destiny. In his classic work, *The Law of Success in Sixteen Lessons*, Napoleon Hill defined concentration as follows:

> **Concentration is the act of focusing the mind upon a given desire until ways and means for its realization have been worked out and successfully put into operation.** (p. 404)

Hill argued that auto-suggestion (imbedding the desires of your imagination into your subconscious mind) and habit are the two pillars upon which concentration, as he defined it, takes root.

Whatever you think and practice repeatedly is stored in your subconscious and acts silently and relentlessly to bring about the realization, in concrete form, of the object of your imagination. Thus, concentration is the habit of fixing in your mind the thoughts, desires and creations of your imagination and insisting on their reality. You can do this because of the DNA of God that is within you and because of the unchanging nature of the universal *Law of Concentration*.

The Apostle Paul made this same point in an even larger context:

> **As it is written: "I have made you a father of many nations." He [Abraham] is our father in the sight of God, in whom he believed—the God who gives life to the dead and calls things that are not as though they were. Against all hope, Abraham in hope believed and so became the father of many nations, just as it had been said to him, "So shall your offspring be."** Romans 4:17, 18 NIV

In this passage, Paul speaks of God's having told Abraham that he was already a father of many nations at a time when Abraham had no children. Just as God spoke to Abraham's future as if it were in present existence, and Abraham believed in and relied on God's pronouncement, so too, can you imagine and speak to your future state as if it were already in existence and believe in and rely on what you have spoken to be actualized in your future.

However, as the biblical passage maintains, in order to concentrate on your desires in a way that will bring results, you must believe that what you desire or what you are creating in your imagination will come to fruition. This principle of calling things not yet in being as though they already exist is content-neutral. In other words, it doesn't matter what the object of the calling is. For example, if you keep calling you sick or inept or clumsy, you will eventually get sick, be inept and become clumsy. If you call you a failure at something, you will most assuredly fail at that thing. On the contrary, if you call you well, you will indeed be well, even if you're sick right now!

What you believe and what you speak about what you believe will determine the content of your future. So the issue of concentration is a double-edged sword. If you concentrate on the bad and the destructive dream, you will have it. If you concentrate on the good and the constructive dream, you will have it. The *Law of Concentration* teaches that you have unfettered freedom and enormous power—the freedom to choose what your life will be and the power to create your own future as you decide it will be.

The real crossroads issue that emerges is whether you wish to take full responsibility for your own life or whether you will choose to behave as if you were powerless. If you choose the former road, the sky is the limit for the dream you create and on which you concentrate. If you choose the latter, you will become the victim you have chosen to be and suffer the consequences of remaining in a state of self-induced powerlessness. Thus, the *Law of Concentration* admonishes you to choose the dream upon which you concentrate carefully, because you will create for yourself and inherit whatever dream you make a habit of meditating on and placing into your subconscious mind.

Overcome the Seven Basic Fears

If you're honest with yourself, you must admit that there are fears that attempt to creep into your consciousness, particularly when you are considering doing something new. These fears have a dual purpose: 1) to keep you from enjoying life now to its fullest; and 2) to lure you into placing them in your subconscious mind through inordinate worry about them in order that they may contribute to your early demise. In order to achieve the greatest level of success possible, you must challenge these fears and conquer them completely. Otherwise, they will rob you of the personal joy and satisfaction of all that you have already accomplished and inhibit your belief that you can achieve an even greater level of personal success in the future. The Seven Basic Fears include: *criticism, ostracism, being alone, losing everything, aging, having debilitating sickness* and *death*.

No one enjoys being criticized, particularly when it is not constructive—and most of the criticism people will give you tends to be less than helpful and more an opportunity for them to share their negative thoughts about you. But you must decide that you cannot let your fear of criticism keep you from your destiny.

I read a story once about a very old man, a very young boy and an old donkey. The three were traveling along on a very long journey with the very old man riding on the back of the old donkey and the very young boy walking along beside the old donkey. When they entered the first town, the townspeople were furious with the very old man for riding on the old donkey and forcing the very young boy to walk beside the old donkey. They said that the old man was cruel and selfish for doing so and complained to him that the very young boy should ride while the very old man should walk. Shaken and dismayed by the harsh criticism of the townspeople, the very old man heeded their advice. He got off the old donkey, placed the very young boy on the donkey and walked beside the old donkey until they reached the next town on their journey.

When they reached the very next town, the townspeople there were outraged that the very young boy had the audacity to ride on the old donkey's back, while the very old man had to walk along beside the old donkey. They screamed at the very young boy and told him he was mean and had no respect for his elders. The very young boy was deeply hurt to the point of tears because of the way the townspeople had criticized him.

But after these two harrowing encounters with townspeople in two different towns, the very old man and the very young boy made a momentous decision: they decided to continue their journey to the next town by walking on foot and carrying the old donkey between them strapped to a pole! Of course, you can imagine the criticism that both old man and young boy had to endure when they reached their next town.

The obvious moral to the story is that people will criticize you whatever you choose to do or not do. If you make or refuse to make decisions based on whether or not you will be criticized, then you will forever have to change whatever course you take whenever the criticism gets too harsh. The antidote to this fear of criticism is to realize that since you're subject to criticism no matter what you do, you need to do whatever you believe will get you to the personal success you seek. You do have a choice: you can be criticized for succeeding or failing. Choose the former!

If you're not careful, your fear of ostracism—being put out, separated from the company of those you admire—can work to thwart your goal of becoming successful. If your sense of who you are requires the approval of others to validate you, then you will make decisions not based on what you believe to be the right or best choices, but on the responses of your social validators. In that case, you're not functioning as a self-determining subject, but rather, as an other-directed object, devoid of the capacity of agency that defines your humanity in a state of freedom.

The fear of being alone is so common in our society that people rush into meaningless and unfulfilling relationships in order to avoid it. In fact, countless people stay in unrewarding and lifeless relationships just so they won't experience being alone. Somewhere deep in the recesses of our brains is this fear of abandonment, of being left alone forever. As with any fear you may experience, the first step is to acknowledge it and seek to discover what in your past caused this fear. Discovering the root cause of this fear is important for gaining the confidence you need to overcome it.

You cannot get to personal success without taking risks—large, life-changing risks. The risks related to moving forward, however, are not as scary or difficult to face and overcome as the risks associated with leaving the comfort zone of your present experience. If you're not careful, the fear of leaving and losing everything you have will keep you from moving into the future where your success lies. In order to take any journey, you must leave where you are to get where you're going.

Your fear of losing everything you know, understand and with which you're familiar rears its ugly head whenever you're required to move away from your past in order to embrace your future. Countless people let this fear of losing everything inhibit them from risking the loss of their current life to gain the benefit of a better, more fulfilling life. Success cannot be achieved without taking significant personal risks—not once, but over and over again.

Fear of aging is not something that crosses the minds of young people: they presume that they will be young forever. But for people over the age of 35, there just may be some momentary, fleeting thoughts about what life will be like when they're older.

Modern medicine has actually heightened the fear of aging for many people. Because medical science has found ways to treat chronic illness and prolong life, many people are worried about outliving their resources. So the thought of aging brings with it the fear of ending up in poverty, regardless of the financial success that may have been part of life when they were younger. You must decide not to worry or fret about what might happen to you when you're 95. You must believe that you will never get old until you decide to be old—which may be when you're 137!

The fear of contracting or inheriting a debilitating sickness is more on the minds of aging people and younger persons who are aware of their family medical history than on people in the population generally. This fear has the ability to limit people's choices for themselves today because they feel tethered to inevitable time-lines in which they see themselves crippled physically, mentally and/or emotionally tomorrow. Consequently, they make what they believe to be "safe" choices—not the choices they would even consider for themselves if the fear of a debilitating sickness were not hanging over their heads.

Like every other fear that stands in the way of your success, this fear must be faced squarely and conquered. You must decide and focus your thoughts on the fact of your long-term health and well-being. You must live your life believing that nothing can keep you from achieving your destiny. Such an attitude will allow you—in the worst case scenario—to adjust to whatever happens to you and keep moving forward into the future, undeterred. Your *Faith* and *Iron Will* are sufficient to get you where you desire to be in life.

Death is probably the biggest fear that most people have. It can come at any moment and it is usually unexpected. There is a real sense in which each of the six fears mentioned before this one have direct, though long, tendrils that connect to your fear of death—the final frontier. For example, your fears of criticism and ostracism are related to your not wanting to experience social death. Your fears of being alone and losing everything mirror your views about the isolation and the "You can't take it with you when you go" reality of physical death. Finally, your fears of aging and debilitating sickness are metaphors for the emotional and psychological death that you view as an inevitable precursor to death itself.

Although a discussion about the fear of death is a difficult one to hold, you must pursue and master it if you seek to be personally successful. Even when you tell yourself that death is a natural part of living it doesn't get at the heart of your fear of death. Fear of death is linked to a deeper fear that you will not be able to accomplish all the things you have planned to do in your life. Therefore, your fear of death is less about the process of dying, and much more about not having enough time to finish what you've started.

When you examine this root cause fear carefully, you will discover that the "dis-ease" the fear causes you is illusory. When you really think about it, you have to admit that you don't really care, deep down, whether you finish or not. If you finish, you'll be looking for your next big project. If you don't finish, you'll have the satisfaction of knowing that death came to you while you were working on the project at hand. In either case, life is the process of living, learning and loving and not necessarily finishing a particular task or project. In this context, finishing is of no importance whatsoever.

You must come to accept the fact that determining to become rich right will not be the cause of your death! Quite the opposite! You will find that your new life will be full of meaning, learning, abundant living, and loving at the very deepest core of your being.

Three Core Leadership Values

Your desire to become an entrepreneur has placed you in a position of leadership. As a leader, you must seek positive and progressive leadership values to guide you as you build your business organization and develop the kinds of relationships with others that will guarantee your success.

There are three Core Leadership Values that come under the rubric of positive leadership: *Self-Mastery*, *Interdependence* and *Reflective Leadership*. A Core Leadership Value is a value or principle that: 1) comes from the inside out; 2) is premised on love and not selfishness; 3) seeks the good of the many rather than the advantage of the few; and 4) is aimed at liberation of body, mind, spirit and emotions.

Self-Mastery is the first and deepest laid foundational building block for positive leadership. It is your taking complete responsibility for your own behavior and determining that you will control your own responses to outside stimuli. This means that you will not blame others for the situation in which you find yourself. You will use your signal endowments of self-awareness, self-knowledge, creativity, imagination, conscience and will-power to be self-determining and proactive. The *Self-Mastery* mindset says, "If it's going to be, it depends on me."

Imagine how great and productive families, communities, businesses and institutions would be if every person associated with them had this attitude of personal responsibility for achieving positive results, and had no inclination to blame others for undesirable outcomes.

Interdependence is the second layer of foundational building block after *Self-Mastery* and it addresses the necessity of developing strategic relationships and understanding their role in creating positive change in a given situation. When you have achieved personal *Self-Mastery*, you realize that you cannot attain maximum effectiveness by dint of your own behaviors and actions alone. You learn that by working in concert with others while being personally responsible for your own actions, a team mentality develops that allows you and every member of the team to contribute to the effort at maximum levels and to experience maximum satisfaction from the process of working together.

Reflective Leadership is the "beyond myself, my family, my community and my organization" third course of foundational building block that requires interdependent personal, familial, community and organizational strategic partners to think and plan together in new ways, using new approaches to create new products, services and solutions that meet needs and effectively address problems. At this foundational level, there is a collective focus on finding solutions to common problems by working together strategically across familial, community and organizational lines to leverage the strengths of each group involved to maximize their collective ability to provide positive leadership in a particular sphere of influence.

There are three foundational principles that accompany the three Core Leadership Values: the *Law of Abundance*, the *Law of Leadership* and the *Law of Change*.

The *Law of Abundance* teaches that you live in a world of abundance, not lack. All the water that has ever been on the planet is still here. All the gold that has ever been on this planet is still here. All the wealth that has been accumulated on this planet is still here.

When you accept the truth of the *Law of Abundance*, you gain two immediate positive effects on your present mindset that are success-oriented. You will become upbeat, grateful and optimistic about the future, and have a positive attitude about and belief in your success.

An *Entrepreneurial Mindset* is your commitment to maximize the personal development and highest and best use of yourself, the resources you receive, and the resources you create.

When you reject the *Law of Abundance*, you gain two immediate negative effects on your present mindset that are failure-oriented. You will become downcast, ungrateful and pessimistic about the future, and have a negative attitude about and belief in your failure as an entrepreneur.

The critical difference between an **Entrepreneurial Mindset** of Abundance and a Mindset of lack is the difference between being positive or negative; productive or wasteful; success-oriented or failure-oriented; having wealth or living in poverty.

The *Law of Leadership* has been defined by many people, based on the particular definition of leadership that they use. Steven Covey defined leadership as communicating to people their inestimable worth and unlimited potential to such an extent that they come to see these qualities in themselves. Others have defined leadership as the function of people who direct, guide or otherwise plan and control the activities of others.

Regardless of one's particular definition of leadership, it is merely influencing the behavior and/or world-view of others within a particular sphere, whether that influence is positive or negative.

Negative leadership is based on raw power and coercion (external force) to maintain itself. Examples include the *power of the gun* (Do what you're told or be killed); the *power of the law* (Do what you're told or be locked up); the *power of economic reprisal* (Do what you're told or you won't be hired, or if already hired, you'll be fired); and the *power of propaganda that preys on fear* (Do what you're told or the terrorists will get you).

On the other hand, positive leadership is based on internal spiritual values (soul power) and operates to empower people, not to dominate them. Examples include the *power of being* (You do what must be done because you have God's DNA—imagination and creativity); *the power of behaving* (You do what must be done because you are free and have the power of choice); the *power of belonging* (You do what must be done because you can cooperate with others and create the Master Mind); and the *power of believing* (You do what must be done because you have faith and the power to see the invisible.)

Political systems, by their very nature, must be external and negative in order to achieve the result of social and political order. Personal systems, by their very nature, must be internal and positive in order to achieve the result of personal wealth. Your challenge is to balance the needs of the external world with the moral and ethical demands of your internal world.

The *Law of Change* teaches that you must change yourself in order to change the world. As Gandhi would put it, "You must be the change you seek." As you change, your character traits will be more fully developed. You will rid yourself of selfishness, greed, arrogance and small-mindedness. Then you will put on a genuine concern for others, a habit of giving freely, an attitude of humility and open-mindedness.

By taking seriously the foundational principles of the *Law of Abundance*, the *Law of Leadership* and the *Law of Change*, you equip yourself to be changed by adopting an Entrepreneurial Mindset so that you can change the world. By observing and living out these three principles, you begin the life-long process of creating a dynamic personal philosophy that will impact you, your family, neighborhood, community and the future of the nation in which you live.

As you continue your journey through the growth stages of leadership, you must remember that mindset is everything, and that an Entrepreneurial Mindset is the necessary and only sufficient beginning place to *maximize your personal development and highest and best use of you, the resources you receive, and the resources you create*. Only an Entrepreneurial Mindset can take you to true success.

Take Small Deliberate Steps

Wherever you are on your life's journey, do what's at your hand to do. Don't sit around waiting for your purpose in life to show up one day. Seek it; pursue it. The way to go after your destiny is to take small deliberate steps to explore what interests you. Some people know what their passion is early in life and are able to run with that passion. But if you happen to have several interests, none of which is so compelling that you would give every other interest up in order to follow one, then simply take each interest, one by one, and take one action each day to explore it.

Your commitment to do just one act every day related to a goal you have set for yourself has powerful significance. You may begin with only one step that you can see ahead of you. But after you take the first step—and sometimes it's the only step you can see to take—another step, not visible to you before you took the first step, will emerge for you to take. You may never be able to fully script your life's journey in advance, but it will always emerge as you move forward, one step at a time. It's like driving through a thick fog that has been forecast to hang around for several days. You can decide to pull your vehicle over to the side of the road and wait until the fog lifts, or you can drive slowly in faith and inch toward your destination. However, unlike a fog, life does not lift in several days—it tends to go on interminably!

So, you are forced to come to grips with the *Law of Faith*. You can't take a step forward in the fog or the dark or into the unknown without having accepted the *Law of Faith* at some level. Somewhere inside of you, you have to believe that what you're doing will turn out right, whether you can see clearly now or not. Living by the *Law of Faith* means simply believing that your life has meaning and purpose, even if you don't know what it is yet. The *Law of Faith* teaches you that you don't have to know—indeed, you cannot know—everything. All you need to know is that if you muster the courage to move ahead, the way will be opened for you to advance. The *Law of Faith* is completely unrelated to your religion or religious preference or nonpreference—it is related to your belief in you and your knowing that you are not alone in the universe. There is help out there, waiting for you to summon it and appropriate it. The biblical definition of the *Law of Faith* is still true:

Now faith is being sure of what we hope for and certain of what we do not see. This is what the ancients were

> **commended for. By faith we understand that the universe was formed at God's command, so that what is seen was not made out of what was visible.** (Hebrews 11: 1-3 NIV)

Every person who has achieved success at any level has believed that whatever his or her goals in life were, they were achievable. In almost every case, great achievement has come to those who moved past criticism and the negative comments of those who kept telling them that what they were after was impossible to attain. What drove them on was their adherence to the *Law of Faith*.

Every solid created thing that you can see with your eyes and touch with your hands is made up of things that you can't see with your eyes or touch with your hands. All matter is made up of elements that are made up of atoms and their three components: protons, neutrons and electrons—none of which is visible to the naked eye. But beyond these building block elements is pure energy! Every new invention, every great idea, every forward advance in science begins in the invisible realm of this pure energy and only later manifests itself in the visible realm. In other words, everything that comes into existence begins with and is brought to its birth through the *Law of Faith*. But, that's just the beginning of the story, as your own life experience and the biblical record maintain:

> **In the same way, faith by itself, if it is not accompanied by action, is dead.** (James 2:17 NIV)

So, the *Law of Faith* teaches you that faith alone is insufficient to get you where you want and need to be. In order for your faith to be effective, you must act—do something—that puts your faith into action. If you say that you have faith that the big chair in the corner can hold your weight, and yet you refuse to sit in the chair, then you don't really believe the chair can hold your weight. You cannot believe yourself into success without taking relevant and timely action to get you there. Your faith is what inspires you to take one step at a time to get to your next destination. But it is your action spurred on by your faith in yourself that takes you to the next destination!

Seven Proven Success Principles

In order to achieve success in any given endeavor you must lay the foundation of completing a solid track record of accomplishment along the way. Small successes in small things lead to larger successes in larger things. By building incremental success into whatever you are doing now, you lay down a history and pattern of success that will follow you into the future. However, it is important to understand that this does not necessarily mean that your failures in small things will result in failing at larger things.

Success is not related to luck or good fortune. It is the result of a process. The process of success includes learning and practicing seven proven success principles. The first of these principles that you must embrace is probably one of the most important lessons you must learn early in your quest to become rich right. You will not know the success you were meant to achieve if you do not *learn from past failures*.

Part of completing a solid track record of personal success is learning from the failures that will inevitably come to you along the road to your ultimate success. Life is of such that you almost never learn from your successes, unless they were unforeseen and purely accidental—many successes have come from failures to achieve intended results. With this minor exception, you can only *learn from your past failures*. If you can learn from your failures, that learning itself lays down a solid track record that will aid you in your future success. You will not find one currently successful person who has not at some point in their career failed utterly at something. To *learn from past failures*, you must understand that part of the process of becoming successful is moving through failure without being discouraged or disheartened to the point of giving up on the dream upon which you've been concentrating. Success is not for the faint of heart, the cowardly in spirit, or the proud. If you are easily intimidated and don't work on strengthening yourself, if you don't have the stomach for being proactive because you are afraid, and if you are too proud to admit mistakes and add to your learning, then you will never know success—maximizing the personal development and highest and best use of yourself, the resources you receive and the resources you create.

To *learn from past failures* is to embrace the teaching that you must be self-confident enough to take risks, but wise enough to assess the risks, consider the rewards and then proceed. If you have done your homework properly, then when you fail you can pinpoint where you went wrong. You may have begun with the wrong assumptions, insufficient facts or dependence on an unreliable source. Wherever you went wrong, whatever you miscalculated in the environment or whoever you misjudged, overvalued or undervalued will become the lesson plan you use to learn, grow and add to your store of wisdom. To *learn from past failures* is never to lose your boldness and self-assured status on the one hand, and always to gain humility and even more fearlessness on the other.

The second success principle that you must develop in order to complete a solid track record of accomplishment is your willingness to *exceed others' expectations regardless of compensation*. It's easier for you to learn from your failures than it is to do more than what you're paid to do. Accordingly, the notion of productivity above and beyond the boundaries of requirement and payment received will not sit well with you unless you are determined to succeed.

This is so for several reasons. When you have worked as an employee for someone else, you are used to selling your time for money and you expect to make the most money in the least amount of time possible. Your "time for money" mindset is not an Entrepreneurial Mindset because it misses the crucial point: entrepreneurial success has nothing to do with exchanging your time for someone else's money, but everything to do with your creation of value that will benefit others.

Another reason why you may not want to embrace the principle that requires that you *exceed others' expectations regardless of compensation* is that somehow you believe that you're entitled to success just because you showed up for work this morning. What you fail to realize is that everybody else also showed up for work this morning—on time, and not late like you are as an employee! News Flash: the new business owner must work harder over longer hours, days, months and years than she or he did as an employee.

A third reason you may not want to *exceed others' expectations regardless of compensation* is that you haven't yet been programmed to go the extra mile, or distance yourself from those around you by the quality, quantity and content of your product or service. The successful entrepreneur must strive to do the work, sell the product or provide the service with increasing skill and effectiveness. In short, only proactive, forward-looking and resourceful people will get the success they claim to be seeking.

When you e*xceed others' expectations regardless of compensation*, you set yourself apart from most people. In fact, you place yourself in a position where you have few—if any—competitors! Having such a posture allows you to own what you do and take pride in it. Under these circumstances, the product or service you provide has personal meaning to you. Also, you seek to improve your own performance and look for ways to upgrade or otherwise improve the entire process of whatever it is in which you're engaged. Your productive and attitudinal mindset change is unmistakably and immediately noticeable to your clients and customers. It sets you apart—even if no one else cares—because you feel better about what you're doing and you're no longer selling your time for money: you're creating value greater than what you could ever receive in dollars and you are adding worth to yourself through your conscientious effort to do what you do to the best of your ability.

Your will and determination to *exceed others' expectations regardless of compensation* causes a radical change in your work ethic and your own sense of self-worth and appreciation of who you are as a productive person who is no longer alienated from the product or service you provide. This behavior of yours, over a consistent period of time, begins to earn you a reputation that will follow you wherever you go. This reputation is the bedrock of the solid track record that you have established that will lead you to your ultimate success.

The third principle of success that you must develop in order to lay a solid track record for success is to *show initiative and leadership*. You begin to do this when you decide to *learn from past failures* and to *exceed others' expectations regardless of compensation*. But you complete the process by being self-directed and self-motivated to plan ahead and set your own goals within the context of your working environment without having been officially authorized or designated to do so.

Now there are definite risks that surface when you *show initiative and leadership*, particularly when it is not an assignment that has been given to you by whoever is supposed to be your boss. If you work for an individual or company that is run top-down, you risk the possibility of being fired rather than promoted. If you decide that the risk is acceptable, then when you're promoted you know you made the right decision. If your ability to *show initiative and leadership* causes you to be fired, then you know you were working for the wrong company. What separates successful people from those who are not is their ability to assume the risk of thinking and behaving like leaders, even when they are positioned as followers.

The fourth principle of success that you must develop is to *exhibit patience and self-control*. It is urgent that this principle be developed and nurtured because there are countless frustrations that act as landmines on your road to success. To *exhibit patience and self-control* is to deactivate these landmines and allow you to continue unharmed by your own words and behaviors in times of stress.

Your *patience* is extremely necessary when you're dealing with people who either do not see the same goal or direction that you see or who see it and make serious efforts to derail the process of moving forward. *Self-control* keeps you from blurting out negative statements that will only make matters worse by closing off any opportunity for negotiation. What you will learn is that many people who seem self-confident, poised and in control of themselves are actually frightened and threatened by any change to their life's routine. So, the thought of change—even for the better—brings out words and behaviors from them that would frustrate anyone who is not afraid or threatened by change. When you *exhibit patience and self-control* with people under these circumstances, you have the opportunity to address the core concerns that drive them in a non-threatening, empathetic manner. Many times, the resistance that people give to new ideas or pathways has more to do with their concerns about the impact on them than it does the merit, usefulness or even necessity of the change. In most cases, your ability to *exhibit patience and self-control* tends to calm people down and provide them the space to slowly open up so that their fears can be alleviated in a way that affirms their dignity and personhood.

What should motivate you to *exhibit patience and self-control* is the reality that you need people to help you achieve your ultimate goal of success. When you *exhibit patience and self-control* and invest the necessary time in building the relationships with people that are required, you are investing in yourself and your own future success.

The fifth principle of success is that you must *excel at cooperation*. Since you realize that you need people to help you achieve the success you're after, it is your responsibility to help others achieve success. In fact, in order to *excel at cooperation*, you must be more cooperative with others than you expect they will be with you. Although this may seem counter-intuitive, it is a prescription that will get you to where you want to go faster than attempting to get there by merely focusing on what you want other people to do for you.

The sixth principle of success that you must develop is to *respect and tolerate others*. To *respect and tolerate others* is simply to come to terms with the fact that your perception of the world—what you call reality—is only your perception of yourself and not of the objective world outside you. So when you *respect and tolerate others*, you're confirming the truth that each person's perception of the world is probably as wacky, crazy and mixed-up as yours. This success principle equips you to understand your own and others' human limitations and your mutually unfounded pride in what you think you know.

What you gain when you *respect and tolerate others* is the satisfaction of knowing that you are sowing the seeds that will allow others to *respect and tolerate you*! The only way that you can demonstrate that you have mastered this principle is to be able to listen to others without judging the content of their message or seeking to prove that their views are wrong and only yours are right.

Listening to others with the intent of merely understanding them will take a great deal of self-discipline. You have been trained to think about what you will say in response to someone while they are still speaking. In such a situation, you're not really listening to what they are saying as much as planning what to say when they're finished speaking; or worse, how you will interrupt them because they're taking too long to make their point!

You will have to practice retraining yourself in order to listen to what a person is saying without thinking about agreeing or disagreeing with what they are saying. You will discover that if you try to mentally put yourself in the place of the person who is speaking to you, you will be better able to understand what they are saying from their point of view. When you're able to clearly indicate that you have heard and understood the speaker's message, the possibility for true dialogue emerges. Even more fruitful than this is the fact that most such hearing encounters of yours will end happily and productively.

Most people you will encounter just want to be heard and understood and are happy enough to walk away with that simple satisfaction. The secret to being able to develop the principle that allows you to *respect and tolerate others* is to pretend to be them trying to talk to you. Just as you wouldn't enjoy talking to someone who must give you their opinion on whether your views have merit or value in their eyes, so too, the person speaking to you doesn't need that kind of response from you. Here is where the Golden Rule comes in. Unless a person specifically asks your opinion, you should only make clear to them that you have heard and understood what they said from their point of view.

The seventh principle of success that will help you complete a solid track record of accomplishment on your way to personal success is to *function with a positive attitude*. The moment you begin your journey toward personal success, there will be obstacles, issues, roadblocks and other impediments that confront you. You can save lots of time, energy and unnecessary heartache if you learn to *function with a positive attitude* despite the negative situations or circumstances that you will inevitably face from time to time. This means that you must control your thought life and focus on only those things and ideas that support, encourage, ennoble, or otherwise lift your spirits.

It is a given that as you travel toward your success destination you will not be able to avoid meeting with unearned animosity, frustration, disappointment, heartache, misunderstanding, confusion, wounded feelings and even betrayal along the way. You must carry the tools that will equip you to encourage yourself during those difficult moments. A good tool kit should include books and CDs by successful entrepreneurs like Napoleon Hill, Bishop T.D. Jakes, John Maxwell, Les Brown, Oprah Winfrey and Tony Robbins, to name a few.

On your self-directed, self-motivated journey toward personal success, you must take responsibility to encourage yourself to such a degree that your personality and attitude are positively charged and you are able to weather the storms of life and the winds of adversity with confidence, joy, hope and optimism. When you are able to experience inner joy, peace and even a weird sense of contentment in the midst of severe trials and testing; when you can still smile and not unleash harsh words and display hostile feelings towards others because of all that has assailed you; when you have time and energy in your own pain to reach out in order to help someone else; then you will know that you have mastered the principle that allows you to *function with a positive attitude*.

The *Law of Speech*

One of the open "secrets" of success that can be of enormous help to you is the *Law of Speech*. The *Law of Speech* says that whatever you speak about yourself, your family, circumstances or situations will come to be because you have God's DNA, His power of speech. Everything that was created by God, with the exception of humankind, was created by God's word—His speech. Speech is more powerful than anything else because it creates out of nothing whatever is consistently spoken.

Speech does not follow religious guidelines or moral laws. It is a universal law that is morally neutral. It is available to you and everyone else. Those who use the law well, prosper. Those who don't use the law well, fail. What this means is that whatever you speak continuously will come into existence, whether the spoken thing is good, bad or indifferent. The *Law of Speech* is one of the central laws that drive systems, product and service innovations. New systems, products and services begin their existence as non-material ideas that people have the courage to speak again and again. Invention begins with speaking the rearrangement of known created things into a new form. It is the power source that God has placed in your hands that allows you to create your own future.

This understanding of the *Law of Speech* teaches you to take positive advantage of the *Law of Speech* to promote your own health and welfare. Such positive speech sets the atmosphere in which all the powers in the universe are unleashed to create for you what it is you continue to speak. But there is more.

The *Law of Speech* requires that you not only speak wholeness, but also commit your active intention—your focused life-force—to the object of your speech. In other words, your speech must be accompanied by specific actions that are aimed at realizing or manifesting what you have spoken. Speech without deeds is useless in the same way that faith without deeds has no value. It is positive speech that must overcome the inertia of the *status quo* to produce the desired new outcome. That is why focused attention (intention) is the catalyst that brings about the birth of the created thing that has been set in motion by positive speech followed by positive action.

You must understand that successful entrepreneurs do not have in their vocabulary such phrases as *I can't*, *it's impossible*, *I don't deserve* and *I don't believe*. These are the limiting negative words that people who don't have the courage to take responsibility for their own lives and livelihoods use to justify their enslavement in a prison of self-loathing, self-doubt and unbelief in their own unlimited possibility as creators, inventors and innovators.

The Threat and Promise of Change

For many people, the most frightening and personally threatening thing, as well as the most exhilarating and personally satisfying thing they can experience in life is change. Change is motion—another definition of what it means to be alive. And since change is the process of being alive, it is both a threat and a promise.

The threat of change is rooted in fear and uncertainty: uncertainty that disorients, causes acute anxiety, and raises disturbing questions about who you are. Therefore, the very notion of change in any quarter threatens to destabilize you, the way you see the world, and how you see yourself in that world. When the threat of change comes toward you, your only question is, "What will become of me?" However, there's another side to the threat of change—its promise. When the promise of change comes toward you, your only question is, "What will I become?"

The promise of change is rooted in your unspoken desire to actually know, understand and unabashedly celebrate who you are, your place and space in the world, and your mission and calling in life. Therefore, the promise of change is your opportunity to experience yourself, others and the world at large first-hand and unmediated by the artificial boundaries and limitations of your upbringing, education and training. The promise of change offers you a new lens through which you can perceive what is going on around you. It provides you with choices that you never imagined you had. It offers opportunities that have been hiding from you in plain sight, and provides you with tools that can move you from where you are to where you'd really rather be.

The promise of change exploits your raw materials of fear and doubt, and from them manufactures products and services that provide you places of safety, areas of knowing and vistas of clarity. The promise of change is the hope that propels you on the quest to live a full, meaningful and productive life that you actually get a chance to enjoy.

Plan Your Estate from a Wealth Perspective

Since your ultimate goal is to not only attain, but also maintain true wealth, you must begin with a wealth mindset. You must hold in your mind the *thought* and in your emotions the *feeling* of being wealthy. You must imagine yourself at the end point: the place where you have abundant, ever-growing material and spiritual resources that you can use to remake and improve the world around you.

It is from this vantage point that you must plan how you will manage your wealth, increase it so that you can freely give to those who need a hand up, and also build a principled legacy of true wealth for your children, grandchildren and future generations of your family.

So, from the very beginning of your quest to get rich right, you must learn the building blocks upon which maintenance of wealth is founded. Then you will be able to plan your future estate as if it were yours right now. This process is called Estate Planning.

Estate Planning is a **Process** that includes **three important elements**:

1. An **inventory is taken** of all your assets, liabilities, family circumstances and your wishes;
2. A **plan is developed** to maximize value, protect assets, and meet your wishes during lifetime and continue them in a thought-through manner at your death; and
3. The **plan is implemented**, using the appropriate legal, business and financial tools and instruments.

You should have an Estate Plan for **three (3) important reasons**:

1. It accomplishes your objectives for your family during your lifetime and beyond;
2. It makes provision for continuation or sale of your business or profession, in case of your disability or death; and
3. It minimizes the tax burden on you and your family.

In order to do state-of-the-art Estate Planning, you will need a team of experts in their given fields. The best Estate Planning Teams are composed of **6 key players**:

1. The Certified Financial Planner;
2. The Estate Planning Attorney;

3. The Certified Public Accountant;
4. The Corporate Trustee;
5. The Life and Disability Agent; and
6. The Property and Casualty Agent.

If you do not have an estate plan that includes a will or living trust, then the law will create an estate plan for you. The entire system of "intestate" succession or "descent and distribution" is set forth by state statute and is too complex for a detailed discussion here.

The bottom line is that without a will or living trust, the law says who will get how much of what you leave behind. The law is inflexible and locked in stone: what it provides may not be what you wanted.

For convenience, brevity and clarity, I will share in a question and answer format some basic Estate Planning concepts along with some of the issues that arise when you don't have a proper Estate Plan:

Q. **What is a personal representative?**

A. Your personal representative is the person who will serve as the primary representative of your estate. You may be more familiar with the terms "executor" or "administrator" for such an individual. An **Executor** is the person named in a Will to be the personal representative. The **administrator** is the person appointed by the court to administer the estate when there is no Will.

Q. **What is "administration" of my estate?**

A. Administration of your estate involves the collection of your assets, payment of your liabilities, and distribution of properties to your beneficiaries or heirs. Administration of an estate is conducted under some degree of court authority and supervision, but a personal representative named in a Will can act with considerable autonomy.

Q. **What is a Trustee?**

A. A Trustee is one to whom property is transferred for the benefit of someone else—the beneficiary. Under present law, a trust that contains well-drafted trustee powers and which uses a professional trustee (Corporate Trustee—a bank or trust company) can solve most problems, and it can assist in creating a suitable Estate Plan that will produce almost any result you desire.

Q. **Is a handwritten Will legally effective?**

A. A handwritten will *may* be a valid holographic will in some states if the signature and material provisions are in the handwriting of the testator. Such a will need not be witnessed or comply with the requirements for an attested will. The holographic will *may* be adequate, but such wills are a fruitful source of litigation, because they have been composed by someone with no legal training.

Q. **Why should my Will be more than one page long?**

A. Your Will could be drafted to be no longer than one page. Indeed, any lawyer can produce an abbreviated will for a relatively small fee. But such a Will may not accomplish your objectives for your beneficiaries. You should have an estate attorney draft your will to cover all the various factual and legal considerations that reasonably may be expected to arise in the future—e.g., having language that handles all the foreseeable "what ifs" that can arise. (Example: You leave your prized diamond collection to your daughter who is married to someone you tolerate, but never liked. If she dies after you, then her husband could end up with the diamonds, **unless** there is a provision in your will to keep the diamonds away from him!)

Q. **Who will raise my minor children during my disability or after my death?**

A. If you are incapacitated or die leaving unmarried minor children, the other parent ordinarily will raise and support them. If the other parent is incapacitated or not living, however, your minor children will require a "guardian." A guardian is an individual who is appointed primarily to care for the person of a minor; the guardian's power over the minor's property is very restricted. You may appoint a guardian for your children in your will. If you fail to do so, the court will make the selection of a guardian. You should assume the responsibility for this important decision, rather than leave it to a judge unfamiliar with your family situation. (The same goes for care of your aged parents who may outlive you!)

Q. **What is community property?**

A. **Louisiana, Texas, New Mexico, Arizona, California, Nevada, Washington, Idaho** and **Wisconsin** are community property states or use a marital property regime very similar in effect as community property. These 9 states use a marital property law scheme that differs from most other states that use the common law scheme. Under the community property system, marital property is deemed to be owned one-half by each spouse, regardless of the legal title to the property. (If you ever lived in a community property jurisdiction while married, you will need an estate lawyer to perform a special review of your estate plan to account for the community property consequences in your present state.)

Q. **How will my estate be taxed at my death?**

A. Your estate may be subject to at least two—and possibly three—taxes: the federal estate tax, a state death tax (called an Inheritance Tax in some states) and possibly a generation-skipping transfer tax. I will confine my discussion to the federal estate tax. The federal estate tax is based on the fair market value of your "gross estate" at the time of your death. At the option of your executor, an alternate valuation date of six months from the date of your death can be used. Your gross estate will include the value of all the property in which you own an interest at the time of your death. Additionally, your gross estate may include property that you do not own, but over which you have retained or received certain rights or powers.

The estate tax scheme provides you with an unlimited "marital deduction" for bequests of property to your surviving spouse. The marital deduction allows gifts between spouses to pass tax free because they are deducted from the value of the gross estate. In order to qualify for the unlimited marital deduction, property must be transferred to the surviving spouse in a fashion that satisfies the technical legal requirements of the statute.

The federal estate tax and the federal gift tax have been combined ("unified") and one progressive set of rates applies. The rates increase as the cumulative total of taxable transfers increases. A unified credit against the gift or estate tax permits the tax-free transfer of a prescribed amount of property.

As the law stands **today,** for people dying between **2018** and **2025** up to **$11.2 million dollars** of assets left by a single person and **$22.4 million dollars** worth of assets for a married couple will pass free of federal estate, gift and generation-skipping taxes. *This is the perfect environment to work your business so you can become wealthy!*

Q. **What's the difference between a Will and a Living Trust?**

A. A Will takes effect only after a person dies, and goes through a court proceeding called "probate" or proving the validity of the will. A Living Trust, on the other hand, takes effect immediately and on the Grantor's death is not subject to probate proceedings.

Q. **How are a Will with testamentary trust and a Revocable Living Trust similar?**

A. For business owners and professionals, well-drafted Wills and Living Trusts are similar in that they both divide the estate of the decedent into two shares: (1) the unified credit exemption that allows $11,200,000 to pass free of the tax; and (2) the unlimited marital deduction that passes to a spouse free of federal estate tax.

Q. **How are a Will with testamentary trust and a Revocable Living Trust different?**

A. The Revocable Living Trust allows the grantor to control his or her assets now, while having in place the mechanism to relinquish that responsibility to others at a later time. In addition, the grantor can appoint a co-trustee or successor trustee to take over management of her assets in case of illness or disability. A Revocable Living Trust can authorize a successor Trustee to pay bills and act as financial manager during the illness or disability of the grantor, which avoids the necessity of a legal proceeding in Orphans' Court to appoint a guardian for the grantor. Because a Revocable Living Trust does not go through probate at the grantor's death, the Trustee can immediately invest Trust assets, pay bills, etc., without having to go to court to get authorization to do so.

The commissions that are payable at death to a fiduciary may be reduced by using a Revocable Living Trust. Even though many banks will charge a one-time trustee's commission for extra duties related to the grantor's death, the charge is frequently less than the same bank's commission for serving as Executor.

A Revocable Living Trust permits a two-part division of the documents necessary to effectuate the estate plan: (1) the Living Trust Agreement, and (2) the pour-over Will. This division permits the will to be a simpler document in that many of the dispositive provisions are already in the Trust.

A Will becomes a public document during probate after the testator's death, while a Revocable Living Trust and its related Pour-Over Will are not public documents. So, if you're a private person and don't want the trust provisions of your Will to become public, then the Revocable Living Trust should appeal to you.

As a business owner and/or a professional, you need the following items—in addition to a Will or Trust—regardless of your present circumstances:

1. A Durable Power of Attorney
2. A Special Health Care Power of Attorney
3. A Health Care Declaration
4. A business Interest Buy-Sell Agreement
5. A Listing of Where Everything Is Located
6. A Letter to Family Outlining Your Wishes

Q. **Why do I need a Durable Power of Attorney?**

A. A durable power of attorney allows you to choose someone whom you trust to handle your affairs should you become physically or mentally disabled. Ask your estate planning attorney about how a "springing durable power of attorney" would operate in your state. In most states, such a document does not permit the person you choose to handle your affairs to act on your behalf unless or until you are disabled.

Q. Why do I need a Health Care Power of Attorney?

A. A Health Care Power of Attorney gives someone you trust the ability to make health care decisions should you be unable to do so yourself. This document helps health care professionals know the kinds of treatment and medical procedures you want and those you do not want. This document avoids court proceedings to determine treatment options.

Q. Why do I need a Health Care Declaration?

A. A Health Care Declaration lets medical providers know your wishes about treatment if you should be in a persistent vegetative state of unconsciousness. This document allows you to choose whether or not you want resuscitation if your heart stops while in a persistent vegetative state, what medications should or should not be used, and declares your right to refuse treatment.

Q. Why do I need a business interest Buy-Sell Agreement?

A. Every business owner should have an agreement prepared that specifies under what circumstances her or his business interest is sold to or bought by a particular person or entity and for what price. These agreements are typically used in partnerships and close corporations. These arrangements are extremely important at the death of a partner in a partnership or of a major shareholder in a family or other closely held corporation. Because we're all living longer, these arrangements are also necessary on the disability or incapacity of a partner or major shareholder.

A sole proprietor must think about how to dispose of or have the business carried on after disability, incapacity or death. Usually, the sole proprietor will change the business form to either a partnership or closely held corporation in order to bring in others who will agree to buy the business in that event.

Q. Why should I make a list of where everything is located?

A. One of the bad things that happens when someone gets ill and can't handle their affairs—or worse, dies suddenly—is that nobody else knows where anything is! Spouses don't know; children don't know; even the family's accountants, lawyers and other helpers don't know. Only the incapacitated or deceased owner knows or knew!

That's why it's urgent that somebody other than you knows the location of things like safe deposit boxes (and keys), bank checking and savings accounts, stocks, bonds, employee benefit plans, insurance policies, wills, trusts, business accounts receivable and payable, orders and/or contracts to be delivered, fulfilled or honored, etc.

Q. **Why should I leave my family a letter stating my wishes?**

A. Most of us laugh and joke with family, tell tall tales, and even share some of our dreams. But we each have a tendency to keep most things that matter to us to ourselves. For some reason, we believe that only we can make the right business and investment decisions. So, we tend to keep the details of what we want for our businesses and families to ourselves.

A letter to your family that shares your hopes and wishes for them, as well as some suggestions for how they should carry on in case of your disability or death will do 3 things: 1) comfort your family; 2) help your family cope; and, 3) share a side of you that not even the closest family member to you knows.

My purpose in sharing the foregoing Estate Planning information is **not** to provide you with Estate Planning advice—you need to consult an Estate Planning attorney to do that—but rather to help you enlarge the way you think about wealth and to motivate you to take responsibility to see that life goes well for you and your family both now and in the future.

Today, Estate Planning is more about your quality of life than it is about your dying: odds are that you will be mentally and/or physically disabled long before you die!

As a spiritually wealthy person who is actively engaged in moving toward manifesting your wealth in material terms, your commitment to learn more about Estate Planning is the action step you will take to demonstrate your concern and care for those you love.

Estate Planning attorneys, life insurance professionals, Certified Public Accountants and Certified Financial Planners often give free seminars and information sessions that you can attend in order to learn more about this important topic.

The Principle-Centered Leadership Paradigm (PCLP)

The Principle-Centered Leadership Paradigm (PCLP) represents "best practices" in leadership training and development—especially for entrepreneurs. It is based on the concept of four distinct leadership levels, each being connected to a key principle. You must study the PCLP and learn it well if you intend to build your business to the point that it earns substantial financial wealth for you and your family.

The first level is *personal* and its key principle is *trustworthiness*. The second level is *interpersonal* and its key principle is *trust*. The third level is *leadership* and its key principle is *empowerment*. The fourth and final level is *organizational* and its key principle is *alignment*.

The PCLP has eight components: *people, self, style, skills, shared vision and principles, structure and systems, strategy,* and *streams*.

The first component of the Principle-Centered Leadership Paradigm is *people* because the PCLP is based on the **effectiveness of people**, rather than the efficiencies of organizational structure, leadership style or systems. **TRUST** is the foundation of all effective relationships and organizations. True empowerment can only take root and grow in a culture of **HIGH TRUST**.

Self is the second and personal level of the PCLP. **Trustworthiness** is a function of **character** and **competence**. Developing your **character** will teach you how to keep promises. Keeping promises makes you a trustworthy person. Developing your **competence** teaches you how to continuously develop your skill sets through on-going training, exposure to new learning and professional development.

Character without **competence** is like having to undergo major heart surgery at the hands of a very caring and courteous, but unskilled cab driver. **Competence** without **character** is like asking for an Enron Corporation or Bernie Madoff fiasco to happen…again and again. **Character** is the inner strength that makes you trustworthy as a moral person, while **competence** is your ability to function in a trustworthy manner as a highly skilled person.

Style is the third component of the PCLP. People who are willing to pay the price of maintaining an **empowerment style of leadership** create more innovation, initiative and commitment, but also more unpredictable behavior. If you persevere and pay the price, over time, you will unleash the potential of people, foster innovation, initiative, self-supervision that respects the individual, and produce desired results better than any high-control leadership style could.

The fourth component of the PCLP is *skills*. Team building, delegation, communication, negotiation and self-management are fundamental to high performance. Fortunately, these skills can be learned and enhanced through continuing education and training. Skills must continually be updated so that your business leadership team and those who follow them have up-to-the-minute **competency** to be highly effective.

The fifth component of the PCLP is *shared values and principles*. Most organizations face a real challenge in getting their people and culture united around a vision and strategy. One of the best ways of bringing about this shared vision is to create a mission statement that is the product of the thinking and work of every person in your organization. A mission statement crafted by everyone will be followed by everyone.

The sixth component of the PCLP is *structure and systems*. The key principle behind structure and systems, along with strategy and streams is **alignment**. With the mission statement in place, the critical imperative for you is to align the 8 components of the Principle-Centered Leadership Paradigm with the principles of the mission statement. The greatest **leverage** and **influence** leaders have is as **mentors** and **models** of the mission statement.

The seventh component of the PCLP is *strategy*. Your organizational strategy should be perfectly aligned with your mission statement, the resources available to you and the prevailing community and business conditions. Your strategy should always be monitored and changed to reflect changing times, conditions and circumstances. In other words, you must be wise enough organizationally to be quick and agile, able to turn and make changes quickly.

The eighth and final component of the PCLP is *streams*. There are many **operational environments** (streams) inside and outside an organization. These environments or streams must be monitored periodically to make sure that your strategy, shared vision, systems and all the other components are all in alignment with the external realities. Also, you must be a wise leader who will read the trends and anticipate changes in the streams to avoid being capsized or left high and dry.

There are six conditions of empowerment: *character, skills, win-win agreement, self-supervision, helpful structure and systems,* and *accountability*.

The first of these conditions is *character*. *Character* is **integrity** (habits aligned with values, words with deeds, expressions with feelings), **maturity** (courage balanced with consideration), **an entrepreneurial**

mindset (maximum personal development and highest and best use of yourself, the resources you receive and the resources you create) and the **knowledge** that you live in a world of abundance where there is no scarcity of resources.

The second of these conditions is *skills*. In order to be empowered you must be skilled in **communication, planning** and **organization** and **synergistic problem-solving**. You must discern the difference between **perception** and **reality** and be able to handle **credibility** and **trust** issues. You must be able to plan and organize your work well and work well with others to solve problems without blaming others or making excuses.

The third condition is working from a *win-win agreement*. A *win-win agreement* is a **contract** between two or more people that spells out 5 specific things:

1. Mutually agreed upon desired **results;**
2. A set of **guidelines** within which to get results;
3. A list of available **resources;**
4. An **accountability** standard; and
5. **Consequences** for getting or not getting results.

The fourth condition is *self-supervision*. Once the win-win agreement or contract has been agreed to, each person who has signed on supervises themselves based on what they agreed to do by a certain date to achieve a defined result or results. When evaluation time comes around, each person evaluates his or her own performance based on what each agreed to do. No excuses, no blaming others.

The fifth condition of empowerment is *helpful structure and systems*. These systems include **strategic planning, organizational structure, job design, communication, budgeting, compensation, information, recruitment, selection, placement, training** and **development**. In such a system, people receive information about their performance directly and can use it to make necessary corrections.

The sixth and final condition of empowerment is *accountability*. In a win-win agreement, **people evaluate themselves**. Since they have a clear, up-front understanding of what results are expected and what criteria are used to assess their performance, they are in the best position to evaluate their performance.

Your attitude as a leader must be helpful, not judgmental. Your role is to be a **coach** to and a **resource** for the people on your team.

In order to make the PCLP work, you must come to grips with the problem of evaluating performance. The problem is that you come to each circumstance in your life with an expectation, a human hope, the embodiment of your desires—what you want out of a situation, whether marriage, family or a business relationship. You have these expectations based on whatever your own past experience has been—good or bad. Your expectations are not necessarily realistic. In fact, they are mostly imaginary. Most of your expectations are imaginary maps—you have notions of what other people **should do** in a given situation. Here is a small sampling of imaginary expectations that you might have. You may expect your significant other to **know** that you need affection, and that you shouldn't have to tell them. You may believe that your boss **should know** that the City didn't plow the snow from your street, and you shouldn't have to explain why you're late to work. Everybody you work with **should know** that you don't like candy, and shouldn't offer you any.

That is why the Performance Agreement is the solution to the problem of **conflicting expectations**. It is the tool for managing expectations. It makes all expectations explicit—puts them all out on the table in writing. The Performance Agreement is a clear, mutual understanding and commitment regarding expectations surrounding roles and goals. It embodies all the expectations of all the parties involved.

There are three (3) parts to a Performance Agreement:

- **Two pre-conditions**—trust and communication
- **Five content elements**—**1)** specified desired results, **2)** set guidelines, **3)** identified available resources, **4)** defined accountability and **5)** determination of consequences for both failure and success
- **Strengthening** of the systems and structure of the organization

The principles of *win-win performance* follow:

- **Specify desired results**, but don't supervise methods and means
- **Go heavy on guidelines,** but light on procedures
- **Mention all available resources,** both inside and outside the organization
- **Involve people** in setting the standards or criteria of acceptable and exceptional performance

- **Maintain trust** and use discernment more than so-called "objective" or "quantitative" measurements to assess results
- **Reach an understanding** of what positive and negative consequences might follow achieving or failing to achieve desired results
- **Make sure the Performance Agreement is reinforced** by organizational structure and systems to stand the test of time

Win-Win Agreements, accountability, self-supervision and *helpful systems and structures* provide the framework in which empowerment becomes possible. It can only become a reality when there is **TRUST** (people trust when **TRUSTWORTHINESS** has been demonstrated consistently over time) and real **COMMUNICATION** (listening to understand, speaking to be understood).

The high-trust culture in which *win-win* can succeed is created by people of integrity, maturity, and an entrepreneurial abundance mentality. People of integrity make and keep promises to themselves and others. People of maturity balance courage with consideration. People with a mentality of abundance assume that there is plenty out there for everyone. They look for third-alternative solutions.

Here are five (5) suggested action steps that you can take:

- 1. **Take inventory** and evaluate personal and organizational effectiveness in each of the six areas (*character, skills, win-win agreement, self-supervision, helpful structure and systems, accountability*);
- 2. **Focus** on creating change in your own personal character and skills and then expand to interdependent areas of influence;
- 3. **Start the process** of creating win-win agreements with Working Group co-chairs and Group members;
- 4. **Work** to create and strengthen supportive systems and structures within your organization;
- 5. **Teach**, exemplify and reinforce.

These action steps are not magic overnight techniques; they are based on sound, time-proven principles of growth and change.

As a leader, you should choose timeless principles as the bedrock for your deep central paradigms of leadership. In time, you will come to understand that natural and spiritual laws in human dimension are just as real as those in physical dimension. You will realize that growth comes from the inside out, so you'll focus first on changing yourself and then on expanding to other areas of influence.

As a principle-centered leader, you will come to understand that growth in yourself and in your organization follows the same process as growth in a garden, so you will work to create the conditions that nurture growth.

As you increase your own capacity and work to integrate correct principles into your life, empowerment will become a vital reality for you and for the people who work with you. Work to empower yourself and others and all of you will become rich right.

Build Your Self-Confidence

You cannot succeed in business or in life without a strong sense of self-confidence. All truly successful entrepreneurs believe in and have great confidence in themselves. This is important because you will encounter more people in your life who lack self-confidence than you will those people who are self-confident. Part of the problem is that most of us have been brought up in families who taught us that self-confidence is a form of pride or arrogance—something to be avoided at all costs. This training has left emotional scars on us that make us feel guilty when we move past our upbringing to make a better life for ourselves and our families.

It's one thing to acknowledge that you may lack self-confidence, and quite another thing to rid yourself from this barrier to your success. So, rather than leave you with a description of the problem, I will offer you the solution—a suggested daily verbal and thinking exercise that will help you to feel and actually become self-confident. If you will find a quiet place and repeat the following affirmations aloud before you go to sleep for a full 30 days, and follow that up by actually *doing* what you promise yourself in the affirmations, you will never lack self-confidence again!

1. I know that I have the ability to achieve the object of my definite purpose in life to become rich right. So, I demand myself to persist toward its attainment by taking definite action, and I promise to take such action.

2. I realize that the thoughts I persistently think about will eventually reproduce themselves in outward physical action and gradually transform themselves into physical reality. Therefore, I promise myself that I will concentrate my thoughts for 30 minutes a day on thinking about the wealthy person I intend to become, and will practice seeing myself now as I will become.

3. I know through the principle of auto-suggestion that any desire that I persistently hold in my mind will eventually come to be through some practical means of obtaining it. So, I will spend 10 minutes a day demanding myself to develop self-confidence.

4. I will write down clearly a description of my definite chief aim in life and I will never stop trying until I develop sufficient self-confidence to attain that aim.

5. I fully realize that no wealth or position can long endure unless built upon truth and justice. Therefore, I will engage in no business or personal transaction which does not benefit all whom it affects. I will succeed by attracting to myself the forces I wish to use and the cooperation of other people. I will induce others to serve me because of my willingness to serve them first. I will eliminate hatred, envy, jealousy, racial bias, selfishness and cynicism in myself by developing love for all humanity, because I know that a negative attitude toward others can never bring me success. I will cause others to believe in me, because I believe in them and in myself.

The Twelve Components of True Wealth

True wealth is much more than financial wealth, although financial well-being is definitely a significant part of it. The first and most important component of true wealth is having *a positive mental attitude*. People who lack a positive mental attitude are miserable, despite whatever money they may have accumulated.

The second and next most important component of true wealth is *sound physical health*. You can lose all your money and recover more than you lost, but if you lose your health you've lost something that may never be regained.

The third component of true wealth is *harmony in human relations*. Harmonious and peaceful relationships, both in the family and then with business associates, lead to good will, a good reputation, cooperation and peace of mind—a personal state of well-being.

The fourth component of true wealth is *freedom from fear*. No fearful person can enjoy life or its perks. Fear robs you of the ability to enjoy life to your fullest capacity and imprisons you in a dark place where there is no peace of mind or joy in being alive.

The fifth component of true wealth is *the hope of future achievement*. It is this component that gets you out of bed every morning to pursue your dream of success. Without hope for the future, you are poverty-stricken even if you are sitting on millions of dollars.

The sixth component of true wealth is *the capacity for applied faith*. The *capacity for applied faith* is your ability to believe in the dream you have for success to such an extent that you actually do something to make it happen. Applied faith is acting to make your dream a reality, while unapplied faith is merely wishing for something to happen for or to you without doing anything to make it happen.

The seventh component of true wealth is *willingness to share your blessings*. You cannot have true wealth if you're stingy and completely self-absorbed. The truly wealthy person gives to and helps others achieve their goals.

The eighth component of true wealth is *to be engaged in a labor of love*. True wealth is only experienced by those who are doing something good that they love. There is nothing in the world more satisfying than being able to do what you love and know that what you are doing is benefitting other people.

The ninth component of true wealth is to *have an open mind on all subjects and toward all people*. The truly wealthy person does not think that the world is only as she believes it to be. She is open to learning from others, listening to their opinions, and not judging them for not seeing the world as she does or believing in the same things as she does. She accepts people for who they are, not for what she believes they ought to be, in her opinion.

The tenth component of true wealth is *complete self-discipline*. The truly wealthy person is self-directed. He is not driven by the whims and demands of other people, but by the goals he has set out to achieve. That is why he has mastered *complete self-discipline*: he refuses to allow any outside influence to distract him from the task of achieving his goals.

The eleventh component of true wealth is *wisdom with which to understand people*. Your life in the world, in your family and in your business consists of interacting with people. To gain true wealth, you must first study the people with whom you interact. But studying them will not give you the wisdom to understand them. The only way you can gain the wisdom to understand people is to put yourself in their place and deal with them from their—not your—point of view.

The twelfth and final component of true wealth is *financial security*. It is not an accident or an oversight that *financial security* is the last component of true wealth. Every component that comes before it paves the way for *financial security* and guarantees that once you have the financial status you desire, you will be able to maintain it by treating everyone by the standard of the Golden Rule.

The Moral and Ethical System of *Maat*

Maat, the moral and ethical system of ancient Kemet (Egypt), has been in existence for over 4000 years. The word *Maat* has multiple meanings, but according to *The Husia*, its sacred text, it essentially means moral and spiritual *rightness* in relation to the Divine, nature, and other humans.[1] It is also an *interrelated order of rightness* which requires right relations with and right behaviors toward the Divine, nature and other humans.

The basic tenets of *Maat*, as set forth in *The Husia*—translated (*Hu*) authoritative utterance (*Sia*) of exceptional insight—include the following:

1. **Humans as the Divine Image of God.** In the Book of Kheti (circa 2140 B.C.E.), it is written: **"Well-cared for is humankind who are the flocks of God....He gave breath of life for their noses. They are His images and came from his body."**[2]

2. **The Dignity of the Human Being.** In *The Husia*, Declarations of Innocence, the *Maatian* prohibition against killing, ordering others to kill, and doing other harm to humans is stressed because as images of God, humans have inherent worthiness and dignity.[3]

3. **Standing Worthy Before God and the People.** One expression of the *Maatian* concept of standing worthy before God and the people as found in *The Husia* is Harkhuf, who testifies: **I was one worthy. One loved of his father, praised by his mother and one whom all his sisters and brothers loved. I gave bread to the hungry, clothes to the naked and brought the boatless to dry land....For I wished to stand well with the Most High God.**[4]

---

[1] Karenga, Maulana. (1994) *Maat, The Moral Ideal in Ancient Egypt: A Study in Classical African Ethics.* Unpublished dissertation, University of Southern California, Los Angeles.
[2] Karenga, Maulana. (1984: 52:VIII) *Selections From the Husia: Sacred Wisdom of Ancient Egypt*, Los Angeles: University of Sankore Press
[3] Karenga, Maulana. (1984: Declarations of Innocence, 110:IV)
[4] *The Husia*, 94, 95: IV.

Worthiness Before Nature. Central to *Maatian* ethics in general and to the environment in particular is the moral obligation to constantly repair, heal and restore the world, making it more beautiful and beneficial than when we inherited it.[5]

4. **The Practice of the Seven Cardinal Virtues of Maat.** *Maat* is defined by the Seven Cardinal Virtues: truth, justice, propriety, harmony, balance, reciprocity and order.

   a. **Truth, Justice.** To say *Maat* is to say truth and justice: **"Speak truth to everyone; let it cling to your speech."**[6] **"Speak truth and do justice. For *Maat* is Mighty. It is great. It endures and it leads one to blessedness...do *Maat* (truth, justice and rightness in general) for the Lord of *Maat*."**[7]

   b. **Propriety.** Propriety requires proper behavior which enhances our relations with each other. **"Do not make your mouth harsh or speak loudly with your tongue. For a loud voice does damage to members of the body like an illness."**[8]

   c. **Harmony.** Living in harmony requires one to listen, hear and respond to others. Ptahhotep speaks of this central virtue of harmony and the role of responsiveness as he says, **"hearing (responsiveness) is better than everything for it creates good will."**[9]

   d. **Reciprocity.** Reciprocity is reciprocal listening, hearing and responding. Of this Ptahhotep says, **"if hearing enters the listener, the listener becomes a hearer...it is the heart (moral sensitivity to others) that causes a person to hear or not to hear."**[10]

   e. **Balance.** The virtue of balance stresses a measured approach to everything, avoiding excesses of any kind.

---

[5] Karenga, Maulana. (1994: 742)
[6] *The Husia*, 66:V.
[7] Id. at 34:VIII.
[8] Id. at 69:VI

[9] Karenga, Maulana. (1994:703)
[10] Id.

"Those who apply the right measure (balance) in all good things are not blamed. The God of just measure has created a balance in order to establish right measure on earth. He placed the heart deep in the body for the right measure (balance) of its owner. Thus, if those who are learned are not balanced, their learning is of little use and a fool who does not know balance does not escape misfortune. Excessive pride and arrogance are the destruction of the owner. But those who are gentle in character create their own fate."[11]

f. **Order.** Spiritual and moral discipline undergirds and makes possible the just and good world. Antef speaks to this eloquently in his Declaration of Virtue:

"I am self-controlled before the angry, patient with the unlearned in order to quell conflict. I am calm, free from hasty acts, anticipating the outcome, expecting what occurs. I am one who counsels in situations of strife, a person who knows which words incite anger. I am considerate when called upon to those who would tell me their concern. I am self-disciplined, kind, considerate, one who comforts the weeper with good words. I am friendly to those who count on me and one who does good to his peers. I am one who is upright in the house of the Lord, who recognizes flattery when it is spoken. I am pleasant, openhanded, a possessor of food who does not hide his face from those in need. I am a friend of the poor and favorable to the have-nots. I am one who feeds the hungry who are needy and one who is openhanded to those who are destitute. I am one who is informed to those who lack knowledge and one who teaches a person what is useful to him or her. I am upright in the house of the pharaoh, one who knows what should be said in every office. I am a listener, one who listens to Maat and who ponders it in the heart. I am one who is pleasant in the

---

[11] *The Husia*, 67: I.

house of his Lord and one who is remembered by reason of his excellent qualities."[12]

5. **The Essentiality of Service, Especially to the Vulnerable.** Harwa, the Grand Steward of the Divine Wife Amenirdis declared, **"I have done what people love and God praises. I was one...who gave bread to the hungry and clothes to the naked. I put an end to pain and erased wrongdoing. I buried the blessed, supported the aged and satisfied the needs of the have-nots. I was a shelter for the child and help to the widow, one who gave rank even to an infant. I did these things knowing their value and knowing their reward from the Lord of *Maat*..."**[13]

6. **Practice of the Declarations of Innocence.** The Declarations of Innocence, often erroneously called "negative confessions," are at the very heart of *Maatian* ethics. On the day of Judgment, one must be able to declare: **"I come to you O Lord. I have brought you righteousness and have done away with Isfet (unrighteousness and the opposite of *Maat*) for you. I have not done evil against people, blasphemed against God, inflicted pain, committed murder or ordered the killing of anyone, cheated, told lies, stolen, robbed, been angry without cause, dealt deceitfully.... I have not been deaf to truth or been blind to injustice...I have done what men and women request and what pleases God. Therefore, let it be said to me: 'Welcome, come in peace.'**[14]

7. **Judgment, Justification and Immortality.** *Maatian* moral theology turns on the concept of *judgment* which carries with it the twin concepts of *justification* and *immortality*. One of the great gifts that ancient Black Africa gave to Judaism, Christianity and Islam is the set of ideas related to judgment after death, reward and punishment, individual responsibility, free will and

---

[12] Id. at 97: X.
[13] Id. at 93: I.
[14] Id. at 111, 112: X.

human worthiness. In the Book of Kheti, *The Husia* says: **"[A] person survives after death and his deeds are set beside him as an allotment...as for one who reaches them (the divine judges) without having done wrong, he will exist in eternity as a divine spirit....Every day is a donation to eternity and even one hour is a contribution to the future. For God knows who works for him."**[15]

This brief summary of the major tenets of the *Maatian* moral, ethical and spiritual tradition is our point of departure as we examine together both the Ten Spiritual Virtues of *Maat* and the Seven Spiritual Principles of *Maat*.

---

[15] Karenga, Maulana. *Maat* (1994: 304, 305).

The Ten Spiritual Virtues of *Maat*

According to ***Maat***, there are **Ten Spiritual Virtues** that define an ethical person, the first of which is *control of thought*. This virtue is especially important for people who seek to be entrepreneurs, because how one *thinks* and what one *thinks* determine what one *does*. In accord with the ancient Kemetic understanding of the importance of controlling one's thoughts, modern business leaders and coaches stress the importance of a successful person's *control of thought* as the key to business and personal success. Modern business leaders are not alone in their urging the necessity of a person's *control of thought*.

Quantum physicists have shown that thoughts are the creative force in the universe. In other words, all created things were once conceived in thought before their appearance in material form. So, if one's thoughts are negative, the universal *Law of Attraction* will draw negative created things, persons and circumstances to that one. On the contrary, if one's thoughts are positive, serving the needs of others and tend toward doing right, then that same universal *Law of Attraction* will draw positive created things, persons and situations into that one's orbit.

The first leadership lesson for the aspiring entrepreneur to learn here is that all thoughts of impossibility, doubt and failure with respect to starting a business—whether starting from scratch or buying a franchise or license—must be eliminated from your mind. You create your own success or failure by what thoughts you allow to stay in your head.

The second leadership lesson you must learn is that you must compete against yourself. Your true opponent does not exist outside yourself. You are the only one who can be your worst enemy by failing to believe in yourself and your capacity to succeed. Fight every thought that comes to you saying, "you can't," "you don't have what it takes," and "don't take the risk."

The second virtue of ***Maat*** is *control of action*. This is significant as a virtue because actions, once taken, cannot be untaken. In human relations, whether personal or business, the words you speak, the deeds you do, and the negative attitude that you display can never be reversed. The old adage, "You can't un-ring the bell," is absolutely true here.

This virtue brings into the foreground the issue of self-discipline. Discipline is enforced obedience. It is bringing your own behaviors under control, regardless of how you may wish to behave in any given stressful situation. Controlling your action is a function of constant practice. If you are used to flying off the handle every time someone makes you angry, then you are out of control. If you want to be a successful entrepreneur and you have serious anger issues, then you are out of business. Your family may, out of love and commitment to you, put up with your bad behavior, but no customer or client will.

If you have trouble keeping your temper in check or cursing before you think, then get help. The art and science of successful entrepreneurs demands self-control in speech and behavior—even body language.

People who are already well-off financially because they have inherited a family fortune can afford to be mean, surly, self-absorbed and rude. Keep in mind, however, that their wealth allows them to live the life they want without succeeding in starting a new business! They are not you, and you are not they!

You are attempting to build wealth for yourself and your family. The only true path for you to succeed in doing this is to treat people with respect, be concerned about them, and serve them to the best of your ability—regardless of how you happen to feel about them personally on any particular day!

So, study to discipline yourself by *controlling your action*—your speaking and behavior. The virtuous successful entrepreneurs work on themselves to bring their thoughts and actions under control so that nothing they think or do becomes a stumbling block to their continued success as a human being and as a wealthy business person.

The third virtue of **Maat** is *steadfastness*—sticking with someone or something until it's completed. You can control your thought and your action, but if you have no *steadfastness*—stick-to-itiveness—you will never fulfill your destiny as a successful entrepreneur.

Steadfastness is the stuff of character that refuses to quit, become discouraged, or otherwise abandon the dream of succeeding in whatever business you have chosen. Life is hard and business is harder. There are no quick fixes or easy roads to the kind of success that lasts over a long period of time.

Just as studies have shown that people who win big lottery amounts are broke within a year after, in the same way, a quick business financial gain—with no more effort put into it than the "luck of the draw"—will always end in business failure. Any business you enter must be nurtured over the long haul by your attention to detail, excellent customer relations and provision of superior goods and/or services.

Another element of *steadfastness* is planning beyond the moment to the future. While you are delivering excellence to your customers today, you must study today how you will exceed your customers' expectations tomorrow. You must constantly improve your product or service and consider your customers' needs past the particular product or service you are currently offering. Thus, *steadfastness* is not only "hanging in there" for today, but also planning improvements and upgrades for tomorrow.

The same *steadfastness* that keeps you from quitting when times are difficult must keep you motivated to never stop improving yourself and the goods or services that your business offers.

The fourth virtue of **Maat** is the *ability to identify with higher ideals*. This is an important virtue for aspiring entrepreneurs because it underscores the reality that true success in business is geared to a higher standard than just making a profit. Although making a profit—and a substantial one—must be the financial goal of the entrepreneur, he or she must resonate with and have an affinity for *identifying with higher ideals*.

To provide people with goods and/or services that add value to their lives is a higher ideal than just making a profit. When an entrepreneur can serve people in a way that enriches their lives, then he or she can experience the satisfaction that comes with rendering such service. This behavior over a consistent period of time is the basis for referrals of business customers from already satisfied consumers. Advertising is necessary and good, but referrals are much better and their results last much longer.

When an entrepreneur chooses to run a business from the place of *identifying with higher ideals*, she or he is investing in people in a way that will come back in ways even more valuable than the money earned through the business transaction. A reputation for excellence, attention to detail, thoroughness or dependability reflects an entrepreneur's functioning with the higher ideals of exceptional service and value to the customer regardless of compensation.

One's *ability to identify with higher ideals* sets one apart as virtuous—a status that is in scarce supply in the marketplace. Consequently, such a virtuous business person has little, if any, competition because consumers care about price, but they care more about the *business experience*. A customer's good business experience with you will speak more volumes than all the ads or commercials you will ever buy.

The fifth virtue of **Maat** is *showing evidence of a mission*. There is more to the virtuous business person than merely earning a living or creating wealth for the family. There must be a sense of mission that is evidenced in the passion one exhibits about what one does. Passion is *feeling*; it is *emotional involvement* in the work undertaken. It is not cold-blooded, but warm-blooded engagement in providing the goods and/or services that one provides.

In a court of law, every fact must be proved by evidence that goes well beyond the speaking or articulation of a particular fact. There must be something more than talk, more than promise, more than the usual hype that accompanies all good advertisements. So, too, the virtuous business person must demonstrate *evidence of a mission* that grounds, rationalizes and supports her or his business activities.

True wealth, in all its aspects, precedes and follows the virtuous business person. That is why the committed entrepreneur who is seeking more than mere financial wealth must develop her or his character to such an extent that the passion for excellence, dependability and service to others becomes the *evidence of a mission* that envelops and consumes her or his life.

The sixth virtue of **Maat** is *evidence of a call to spiritual order*. *Spiritual order* is that state of being that is fully aware that one cannot live for oneself and family alone: one has a call to destiny that goes beyond one's own private sphere of living. One has the *obligation* and *responsibility* to live a virtuous life that impacts, influences and encourages others to follow suit.

The old adage, "To whom much is given, much is required," is in play here. Every successful entrepreneur is a leader, whether she or he understands that or not. A leader is someone who is followed. People who wish to become successful follow the lead of those they believe to be successful. Because people will be watching you as you develop into a highly successful individual, you must be a good example for them to follow.

You cannot afford to be selfish, stingy or rude if you intend to obtain true wealth. You must show love, compassion, empathy and personal discipline. You cannot live the kind of life that you've seen some rich people live. Your life must have meaning, purpose and *spiritual order*. True wealth and long-term profitability can never reside in a person who lives a dissolute life—a life wasted in self-indulgence and self-absorption.

The seventh virtue of **Maat** is *freedom from resentment*. It's amazing how many people are stuck in an undesirable space in life simply because of their *resentment* toward other people: a parent, a sibling, a former lover, a current colleague or fellow worker, to name just a few. In too many cases, *resentment* is the excuse unsuccessful people use to justify their failures in life.

They love to blame others for what is actually their own inadequacy. They will talk about the father who abandoned them, the mother who didn't love them, the teacher who discouraged them, the close friend or lover who betrayed them, and on and on.

To have *freedom from resentment* is to be so self-directed that you will not allow any person or circumstance to keep you from attaining the goals you have set for yourself. *Freedom from resentment* provides you a platform from which you can create, innovate, and focus on your positive future, rather than to stay mired in your troubled past or hurtful present. As a virtuous, highly successful entrepreneur, you will learn that the pure success you earn in your life is far sweeter than any bad feelings you could have harbored or any acts of revenge you could have carried out.

The way to gain *freedom from resentment* is to make yourself grow large enough internally to forgive the people who have wronged, betrayed or otherwise treated you unfairly. Forgiveness is not easy, but it is easier than holding on to resentment, because *resentment* traps and holds you, while forgiveness sets you free to become all you can be.

Along the road to economic prosperity there will be potholes and other rough spots that are designed to discourage and waylay you as you seek after true wealth—wealth that includes financial success. Remember that the *Law of Attraction* will bring you whatever you focus on in your mind. Don't waste time and energy on negative thoughts of *resentment* because they will attract more negative things and people to your life. Forgive those who have wronged you, and the people whom you have wronged will forgive you.

The eighth virtue of **Maat** is *confidence in the power of the master (teacher)*. This virtue is important because you do not know everything there is to know about the business you will choose to begin from scratch or purchase as a franchise or licensee. You must learn the ropes from somebody and you will not learn what you need to know if you have no confidence in the power of the person who is teaching you what you need to know about the business.

The virtue that is hiding behind this eighth virtue is that of *humility*. A prideful person has difficulty acknowledging that anyone knows more than she or he about anything. Consequently, there are many entrepreneurs struggling in business because they refuse to learn from those more experienced than they, or to take their advice.

It's not always pride that can make you leery about having *confidence in the power of the master (teacher)*, sometimes it's your bad past experience with a so-called teacher who turned out to be incompetent at best or a shyster at worst. That is why you must check out carefully the company or the business you choose to invest in to make sure that the people who will be teaching you the ropes know what they are doing.

The ninth virtue of **Maat** is *confidence in your own ability*. Without *confidence in your own ability*, you can never achieve personal and business success. The power of who you are as a person created in the image and likeness of God cannot be unleashed until you believe in yourself. This belief in the self and the self's ability to succeed is an acknowledgement of the power of God's DNA at work within you.

The true atheist is not the one who disclaims belief in the Deity who created the universe and humankind, but the one who refuses to believe in the self created by God. To denigrate your own ability is to practice false humility—the attempt to appear humble, when in fact, you are insulting the God who created you.

You are what and who you persistently think and believe you are. If you practice seeing yourself and *feeling* yourself to be successful, that is what you will ultimately become. *Confidence in your own ability* is the driver of your success, just as belief that you will fail is the driver of your failure.

The tenth virtue of **Maat** is *preparation for initiation*. In essence, this tenth virtue is the launching pad from which you will make the decision to commit to the business choice you have made, and give your whole self to its pursuit.

Preparation for initiation is your decision to move away from talking about going into business for yourself and taking the necessary action to do so. It is moving away from simply thinking about going into business and actually doing it. *Preparation for initiation* is moving away from merely asking the theoretical questions related to going into business and embracing the practical reality of setting up shop.

The first step in your *preparation for initiation* is to save the money you need to get started in business while you do a thorough check—your due diligence—of the business opportunities available to you. The second step is to engage a seasoned professional who is qualified to assist you during your decision-making process.

The Seven Spiritual Principles of *Maat*

The Primacy of *Truth*

Truth is reality in itself, not any perception of or reasoning about it. Its existence begins in spiritual form prior to its manifestation in material form. Anything that is not predicated upon truth is *unreality*—a lie.

That is why telling the *truth* to self first and then to family, colleagues and business associates is imperative for the honest entrepreneur who is seeking true wealth. Building relationships of trust demand *truth* as the foundation of trustworthiness. The only way a person will come to trust you is if they find that you always tell the *truth*, even if it hurts you.

When it comes to making critical decisions that will impact profits over long periods of time, wise business leaders look for trustworthy associates whom they know will tell them the *truth* and stand by their commitments.

There are many entrepreneurs who cut corners, promise more than they can deliver, and function based on their perception of taking advantage of others. They may appear to succeed over the short term, but eventually they are exposed as the untrustworthy, untruthful and unreliable people they really are.

Truth is a rare commodity that is found only in the best entrepreneurs who love themselves to such an extent that they show love to others by fair dealing, win-win diplomacy and honest *truth* telling in business deals and in personal relationships.

The Importance of *Justice*

Justice is God's definition of what is right. It is not based on any partisan religious view or political persuasion, but rather on the Golden Rule. It is important for entrepreneurs who want to function in a virtuous manner to practice *justice* in all their business and interpersonal dealings.

In the realm of business, *justice* means that you commit that you will not enter any deal that is disadvantageous to any person or entity involved in the venture. It means that all the details of the deal will be set forth fully and that pains are taken to make sure that everyone involved is clear about what work, activity, product or service is expected from each, and how, at what time and under what specific circumstances each will receive compensation for performance or no or limited compensation for non-performance.

The most direct way to ensure *justice* in a business deal is to create a Performance Contract that spells out clearly and succinctly what is to be done by whom, when, where and how it is to be delivered, and the consequences for both performance and non-performance. A properly written Performance Agreement will minimize to zero litigation and the waste of time and money that occurs when business partners disagree over the terms and conditions of a given deal.

The virtuous entrepreneur who adheres to fair dealing and functioning with *justice* in all personal and business dealings will always gain true wealth and maintain financial security for a lifetime.

The Urgency of *Righteousness*

Righteousness is right standing with God that is evidenced by your right treatment of people, animals, plants, and the planet. ***Righteousness*** is not related to your religious or non-religious beliefs: it is predicated solely on what you actually *do*—your performance—not what you say you believe.

The financial destiny of a virtuous entrepreneur is to become wealthy enough to make a tremendous positive impact on the lives of people and to exercise economic power such that the world becomes a better place to live.

Righteousness is urgent because those who gain wealth have an obligation to function from right motives in order to reach right ends that benefit society at large. To gain wealth solely to subjugate others is a misappropriation of the gift of wealth and a crime against humanity.

It is not money or wealth that is sinful: it is the selfish love of money or wealth that causes unrighteous people to write laws that oppress and diminish people, despoil the planet for profit, and reap unjust gain in the process.

As you enter the economic world of entrepreneurship, you have a decision to make. Will you decide to follow the narrow path of *righteousness* or the wide road of unrighteousness? You can become part of the world's problem or part of the world's solution. Which way will you choose?

The Necessity of *Balance*

Balance is maintaining and manifesting a healthy understanding of duality: wrong is balanced by right; good by evil; south by north; one's perception by another's. One of the hardest leadership lessons to learn is that there is nothing in our experience that is all wrong or all right. What makes this such a hard lesson to learn is our misguided belief that our perception of the world is reality. The inconvenient **truth** is that our perception of the world is not reality at all, but merely our perception of ourselves.

Each of us creates from our individual perceptions of the world the picture in our minds that we call reality. Based on our individual notions of reality, we develop a code that we use to explain what we perceive around us. We decide what is good, what is bad, what is proper, what is improper—all based on what we were told by our parents as children and what we have learned on our own through "good" and "bad" personal experiences.

Your desire to be a successful entrepreneur catapults you to the status of a leader in society. You will lead your company, co-lead your family, and have considerable input in whatever organizations or associations to which you belong. Because you are a leader, you have a moral obligation to move beyond the ignorant opinions and self-serving partisan views held by most people with whom you currently associate, and commit yourself to learning all you can about everything that touches you and your family. This is necessary because you cannot be a true leader and a *thought follower* at the same time. If you stay in that position, you are merely a client or object—someone's puppet—to be used and manipulated as others see fit. If you take your rightful place as a *thought leader*, you are functioning as a subject or agent—a person operating in freedom.

The only way you can function properly as a thought leader is to see the pros and cons of every point of view without siding with one view or another, and to look for, find or create the third way—the **balanced** view that only a forward-thinking entrepreneur has the capacity to promulgate. Lead from **balance**; serve others from **balance**; and innovate, improve and create from **balance**.

The Requirement of *Harmony*

Harmony is undisturbed peace, trust and good will between and among two or more people who are either living together, doing business together or working together on a social or community project. **Harmony** is third on the list of the top 12 conditions that are required for gaining wealth. This is so because acquiring wealth is not an individual sport, but a group activity.

Without the concerted and harmonious efforts of a dedicated group, wealth is impossible to amass in the U.S. in the 21st century. What this means is that wealth is acquired these days by groups of people who work together and share in the profits from their labor as owners of a collective enterprise.

Andrew Carnegie, Charles Schwab, Henry Ford, J. P. Morgan—and the list goes on—all got wealthy together because they each assisted the other to amass wealth. They succeeded because they cooperated together in *harmony*. Each chose an industry to thrive in that did not compete with the others' business interests. Because there was no competition between their Master Mind group they could whole-heartedly help each other in an unselfish way.

As you move into owning your own business, find out what other businesses are compatible with yours and make strong friendships with owners of those businesses. As you cooperate in *harmony* with owners of businesses that are not in competition with you, you are creating a Master Mind that will provide the catalyst for the quickest and most honorable way to get rich right.

The Need for *Order*

Order is the evidence of a disciplined lifestyle that refuses to tolerate clutter, distraction and dysfunction. It is the ground upon which the virtuous entrepreneur builds her business. *Order* is the house in which your creativity and innovation live. ***Order*** is important because without it chaos reigns. Chaos is the enemy of ***order*** and the author of confusion. ***Order*** is not just the absence of chaos, but the sign and signal that mark you as a person who lives with intention.

Order and intention immediately evoke the mental picture of a progression that proceeds in one-step-at-a-time fashion. Such a progression is a definite plan of action. Without a plan, your intention has no definite object upon which to focus. If you have no definite object upon which to focus, the *Law of Attraction* will bring you more of the same—confusion, chaos and failure.

If you want to be successful, you must concentrate on a definite goal and give yourself entirely to its accomplishment by making a definite plan to achieve that goal. ***Order*** in your life is the clear space in which you are able to do the planning you need to do in order to succeed in life and in business to the point of getting rich right.

The *Law of Reciprocity*

The *Law of Reciprocity* (sometimes called the *Law of Retribution*) has two parts: 1) you reap what you sow; and 2) you must share what you reap with others. In terms of its first part, the *Law of Reciprocity* teaches you to take the gifts, talents and skills you already have and invest them wisely so that you can reap a harvest of true wealth.

In terms of its second part, the *Law of Reciprocity* makes a demand on you that you not only share the harvest of the good you have sown with others, but also leave more on the planet than you inherited. Thus, the *Law of Reciprocity* requires you to build wealth so that you can give back more than you received at birth.

This teaches you that your financial goals must be larger than making a comfortable living for your family. You must think beyond your immediate family and consider others outside that tiny little clique. If you allow yourself to think small, you will receive little—in fact, you will receive less than your own family will need. You must think big and plan big to be a blessing to many people by building up a business or an industry that will be a base of economic good for many people.

You must begin to think about employing people and paying them a living wage that will allow them to provide for their families. Not everyone has the ability to be a successful entrepreneur. But, as an aspiring entrepreneur, you must begin to accept the challenge of creating wealth significant enough to provide training, employment and benefits to those who will be working for your company.

Once you understand the demands of the universal *Law of Reciprocity*, you cannot again speak about not wanting to be rich. Indeed, you are obligated by the *Law of Reciprocity* to become rich—not for yourself, but for others who do not have the entrepreneurial skills and abilities that you have. Building wealth is not a personal, selfish thing: it is a public, unselfish thing that can add value to the lives of countless people. Just own it! It is your destiny.

Jesus' A.S.K. Principles

"Ask and it will be given to you; seek and you will find; knock and the door will be opened to you. For everyone who asks receives; the one who seeks finds; and to the one who knocks, the door will be opened. "Which of you, if your son asks for bread, will give him a stone? Or if he asks for a fish, will give him a snake? If you, then, though you are evil, know how to give good gifts to your children, how much more will your Father in heaven give good gifts to those who ask him! So in everything, do to others what you would have them do to you, for this sums up the Law and the Prophets. Matthew 7:7-12 NIV

Don't let the seeming simplicity of Jesus' words lull you into a mindless stupor. The very Son of God is the Teacher Who is sharing with you the secret of how to get rich right. Behind His words, however, lurks a condition that may keep you from actually hearing, receiving and applying what He is teaching here—your lack of humility.

Jesus teaches that in order to get anything that you want in life, you must first ask God for it. If you lack humility and take the view that you can get what you want without God's help, then you will be too proud, arrogant and stupid to open your mouth and heart and humble yourself to ask God for what you want. Instead, you will get it on your own, only to find that what you end up with is gravel in your mouth.

Humility is having the grace (and the sense) to willingly and intentionally (with deep respect) bow before the Creator and Sustainer of the universe and acknowledge that He is the only One capable of meeting whatever need or desire you have. Humility is an internal mindset, not an external act that people can see. Nobody knows what a humble person looks like. You may think that a person is humble because he or she acts in some subservient or obsequious manner in a given situation. Humility is more internal and Godward, than external and peopleward behavior.

What Jesus teaches is not a prescription for becoming religious or engaging in synagogue, church or mosque-related religious activity. There are no strings attached, rules to follow or conditions to be met at this stage. Jesus simply says "Ask and it will be given to you." The conditions will come later—but even then, they will not be rules of religious engagement.

After you have asked God for what you want, you must expect to receive it. Your expectation of receiving what you have asked for is demonstrated by your looking for it all around you. You must be so sure that you will receive it that you keep that thing you desire in your mind to such an extent that you are always looking with expectancy to see it when it materializes.

Jesus then says, "knock and the door will be opened to you." This is your cue to be persistent. Once you have asked and then you have looked for what you want, then nothing is left but to persist in asking, seeking and knocking (A.S.K.) until what you desire materializes.

Knowing in advance that you would eventually lose heart when what you ask, seek and knock for doesn't materialize right away, Jesus goes on to assure you that **everyone** who asks, seeks and knocks will get what they're after. You don't have to be a holy person, a religious person or even a good person to get what you ask, seek and knock for. You are guaranteed to get what you want if you will persist and not give up.

Jesus explicitly states the reason why you must get what you ask, seek and knock for: God is good, holy and a much better heavenly Father than any earthly father who is steeped in selfishness and evil. He points out that even a sinful and evil earthly father wouldn't give his own child a stone if that child had asked him for bread. Neither would an earthly father give that same child a snake if the child had asked for some fish.

So, Jesus says, "If you, then, though you are evil, know how to give good gifts to your children, how much more will your Father in heaven give good gifts to those who ask him!" Note that Jesus uses this teaching opportunity to teach that **everyone** is a child of God and has been given access to God the Father without having to do one thing more. This is revolutionary because Jesus forever removed the "us versus them" mentality that is so prevalent in organized and disorganized religion.

After announcing all of the foregoing, Jesus states the one simple condition that you must meet that will guarantee your continued success *after* you get what you asked for: **"So in everything, do to others what you would have them do to you, for this sums up the Law and the Prophets."** According to Jesus, the very Son of God, if you treat everybody the way you would want them to treat you, you have fulfilled what God requires. Simply put, doing to and for others what you want them to do to and for you is all the religion you will ever need!

Jesus' Teaching on Emotionalizing Your Intention

"Have faith in God," Jesus answered. "Truly I tell you, if anyone says to this mountain, 'Go, throw yourself into the sea,' and does not doubt in their heart but believes that what they say will happen, it will be done for them. Therefore I tell you, whatever you ask for in prayer, believe that you have received it, and it will be yours. And when you stand praying, if you hold anything against anyone, forgive them, so that your Father in heaven may forgive you your sins." Mark 11:22-24 NIV

Once you begin the process of asking, seeking and knocking (A.S.K) in order to reach your goal, you must then believe that you will receive what you asked for. This means that you must take seriously the notion that you are God's child. Since God is All Powerful, then at the very least, you, as God's child, have direct access to that All Powerful power who happens to be your Heavenly Father. The very fact that Jesus admonishes you to ask God directly and unmediated for what you want is proof of this.

Jesus' teaching that you are God's child as of right and not because you had a religious experience or decided to adhere to the "correct" religious doctrine and dogma was so revolutionary that the religious establishment of His day saw Him as a threat to their power and went about to kill Him.

Jesus is still a real threat to "religious middle-men" today because He teaches you to bypass them completely and go directly to your Father God for whatever you desire.

It is not surprising, then, that today's religious establishment is very much at odds with the teaching of Jesus because when you obey what Jesus teaches, you are free from their control and are not subject to their petty religious regulations, rituals and rules.

When you are in any kind of bondage—whether religious, secular or otherwise—you will tend to *emotionalize* your connection to that bondage. Consequently your emotional energy is sabotaged and sapped to such an extent that you have none left to focus on acquiring the true wealth that you seek.

This leads to the conclusion that you must be free from every kind of bondage—physical, spiritual, psychological, mental and emotional—in order to direct your emotions toward achieving your goal.

Jesus makes clear in the above passage that your unwavering faith in God will put you in such a position of power that you will be able to accomplish seemingly impossible things, like telling a mountain to go take a hike. Of course, you must believe beyond a shadow of doubt that what you have said will happen, will actually happen for you. And the only way that you can *know* that you believe beyond a shadow of doubt is to *feel*—i.e., emotionalize your mental belief—that you believe beyond a shadow of doubt.

This open, but hidden to most, secret—believing (and thereby *feeling*) that what you say will come to pass—is the lynch pin upon which your success must hang. It is the combination of the *Law of Speech* (what you say will be) and the *Law of Faith* (belief that what you say will be) that will take you to your desired destination, but doubt (unbelief) will only destroy your destiny.

That is why Jesus teaches, "Therefore I tell you, whatever you ask for in prayer, believe that you have received it, and it will be yours." The fact that you must believe that you have *already* received what you asked for requires that you transfer your mental intention into your *feeling* emotions. It is not sufficient that you give mental assent to the notion that you *will get* rich right. You must *feel* that you *are now* rich right.

In order to move from rationality to emotionality, you must imagine what it *feels* like to be successful in business to the point of becoming wealthy. You must practice this by picturing in your mind how you would behave, live and give if you now possessed the wealth you seek in the future. You must put a great deal of energy into this and awaken the little child within you who has the capacity to believe and *feel* that the apparently impossible is possible with God and guaranteed to happen for you. In fact, you must do this until it becomes such an obsession with you that you actually begin to behave, live and give *now* as if you already had the wealth you desire.

This means using your imagination to pretend that you are already where you want to be. Once you persist in this "pretend mindset," you will begin to *feel* like you're already wealthy. Your *feeling* presently wealthy is proof that you have already received what you asked for in spiritual terms. It is just a matter of time before what you have already received spiritually is actualized materially.

It takes passion—*feeling*—to move a focused thought out of the mind and into the emotions. Only in the emotions can a thought be transmuted (changed) from mental energy to spiritual energy that eventually manifests itself into physical materiality.

Just as in the case of His A.S.K. principles, Jesus sets forth a condition that you must meet: "And when you stand praying, if you hold anything against anyone, forgive them, so that your Father in heaven may forgive you your sins."

Whenever you ask, seek and knock for anything, you are praying. All that Jesus requires of you is that you forgive people who wrong you, so that God can forgive you for wronging Him and other people.

Sinning is a fact of life. Not even you, even in your spirituality, are free from sin—missing the mark, getting it wrong, making fallacious judgments about people without having all the facts. Welcome to the human family! Since Jesus took on all the sin of all the people on this planet, past, present and future—including yours and mine—and forgave it on His cross, He merely asks that you forgive people who wrong you so that you can be forgiven for wronging others.

This is Jesus' only *quid pro quo* demand for getting what you desire. It is not a religious demand, but a restatement of the Golden Rule. Treat, love and do good to other people in the same manner that you desire them to treat, love and do good to you. But forgive other people as you desire God, the Righteous Judge, to forgive you. Thus, Jesus puts the measuring yardstick in your hands. Your behavior toward others will determine God's behavior toward you now and on into eternity.

It's not complicated. Follow Jesus' simple prescription and you will be well on your way to get rich right and stay rich right!

Jesus' Teaching on Kingdom Entrepreneurship

According to Jesus, kingdom entrepreneurship has a natural dimension, a spiritual dimension and a transformational dimension—three distinct dimensions that require three distinct access cards. Because kingdom entrepreneurship is three-dimensional, no one dimension, by itself, can sufficiently define it. So, in order to get a handle on kingdom entrepreneurship, you must examine all three dimensions. Let's start with the description of the natural dimension of kingdom entrepreneurship that Jesus laid out for you in the parable of the gold talents at Matthew 25:14-30.

In that passage of Scripture, Jesus tells you that the natural dimension of kingdom entrepreneurship is like a man who was going on a journey who called his own servants—his stewards—and gave them his property.

He gave the first steward five talents or more than five thousand dollars, he gave the second steward over two thousand dollars, and he gave the third steward over one thousand dollars. The first two stewards got busy and doubled their master's money. They took risks. They had no guarantee that they would be able to double their master's money when they started out. In fact, because they engaged in the risky business of market trading, they both faced the possibility of losing everything that had been entrusted to them by their master. But even though they were faced with the fear of possibly losing everything that belonged to their master, they traded anyway and were able to double their master's money.

On the other hand, the third steward who was given only one thousand dollars was so afraid of the possibility of losing everything he had been given, that he hid the money and didn't do anything with it. So when the master returned, the first two stewards reported that they had doubled his money. The master praised them, called them good and trustworthy stewards, and promoted them to have responsibility over even more of his property.

When the third steward came to the master to give his report, he called the master a harsh, unscrupulous business man who took what didn't belong to him. And he used his foul opinion of his master as his excuse for being afraid and hiding his master's money. The master called the third steward a wicked and lazy steward and told him that if he really believed that he was such a ruthless man, he should have put his money in the bank, so that at least the master would have earned some interest on his money.

The master ordered that the thousand dollars be taken from the wicked, lazy steward and given to the steward who had ten talents. Then he ordered that the wicked and lazy steward be thrown into the outer darkness, where there would be weeping and gnashing of teeth.

So now, based on this description by Jesus of the natural dimension of kingdom entrepreneurship, you can begin to apply His teaching to yourself. You are a kingdom entrepreneur because you have been given property, gifts, abilities and the power to get wealth by God. You can also begin to see that God has an expectation of you: He expects that you will overcome your fear in order to maximize what God has entrusted to you.

Jesus' description of the spiritual dimension of kingdom entrepreneurship is found in His parable of the Good Samaritan in the gospel of Luke 10:30-37. You are probably familiar with this parable, but let me give you the modern 21st century "in the hood" version.

There was a woman who was going down Germantown Avenue from Chestnut Hill (a prosperous neighborhood) to North Philly (a poor neighborhood), when she fell into the hands of robbers who carjacked her, stripped her of her clothes, beat and raped her, and went away, leaving her half dead. A preacher who was practicing her sermon on love came down that same Avenue, saw the condition of the woman, kept on preaching love to herself and then passed by on the other side. A choir member on her way to the preacher's church for choir rehearsal was singing Amazing Grace as she also came down Germantown Avenue where the woman was, saw the condition of the woman, kept on singing Amazing Grace to herself, and she, too, passed by on the other side.

Finally, an HIV-positive lesbian woman who never went to church because she was not welcome in the preacher's church, nor would the choir member ever sing Amazing Grace to her because the singer didn't believe Amazing Grace could stretch that far, came along the Avenue to where the wounded woman was, saw her condition, and bandaged up her wounds, pouring in some wine and oil that she happened to have in her back pocket. Then she put the wounded woman in her own car without worrying about whether the woman's blood would stain her car seat. She took the woman to Temple University Hospital and took care of her that night. The next day the HIV-positive lesbian woman gave the hospital her credit card and asked the hospital to take care of the wounded woman and put the charges on her card until she returned. And she authorized the hospital administrator to charge her account for whatever other expense came up in caring for the woman.

What Jesus taught here as the spiritual dimension of kingdom entrepreneurship is that God associates with, is accepting of, and shows approval for a kingdom entrepreneur who is a neighbor, though not a Christian or a church member, but who does the will of God that Christians and church members often refuse to do. For just as in Jesus' day most Jews would not associate with, be accepting of, or show approval for Samaritans, so today too many religious people of all stripes will not associate with, be accepting of, or show approval for LGBTQ people and people who are living with the devastating affects and effects that HIV and AIDS are still having in communities.

This applies to you as a kingdom entrepreneur. At your spiritual core, you must understand and accept the fact that you cannot use your political, social or religious "holier than thou" beliefs to deter you from caring for any person you encounter who is hurting. You are not called to judge—i.e., condemn—people, but to do your part to help them as best you can.

Jesus' description of the transformational dimension of kingdom entrepreneurship is found at Luke 4:18-19, where Jesus describes his own role as a kingdom entrepreneur:

> **The Spirit of the Lord is upon me, because he has anointed me to bring good news to the poor. He has sent me to proclaim release to the captives and recovery of sight to the blind, to let the oppressed go free, to proclaim the year of the Lord's favor."**

In this passage of Scripture, Jesus describes the transformational dimension of kingdom entrepreneurship as your engagement in His anointing to liberate the oppressed and bring the good news of social justice to the poor. So, let's sum up Jesus' three-dimensional definition of kingdom entrepreneurship.

Jesus teaches you that the natural dimension of your role as a kingdom entrepreneur requires that you move past fear to be productive and faithful, maximizing the natural resources that God has given you. The spiritual dimension of your role as a kingdom entrepreneur is to choose to be a neighbor who will not pass by any hurting person on the avenue of life without going where that person is to help. And the transformational dimension of your role as a kingdom entrepreneur is to commit to follow Jesus in his ministry to liberate the oppressed from their exploited condition and to seek social justice that will release poor people from poverty.

The way you apply this to your life is to be intentional about paying your workers a living wage—enough money to support their families—and to treat them with respect.

So with these three dimensions of what it means to be a kingdom entrepreneur in your mind, you're ready to discover the secrets related to your access cards to each of the dimensions of kingdom entrepreneurship. A kingdom access card opens up your understanding of a mystery or secret of the kingdom of God.

But, before this can occur, you must know that for every kingdom access card, there is a kingdom rule, a kingdom guideline, and a kingdom leadership lesson connected to it. A kingdom rule explains what God requires of you in his kingdom right here on this earth. A kingdom guideline shows you how to follow God's kingdom rules. Finally, a kingdom leadership lesson teaches you how to take what you've learned about the kingdom of God and put it into practice in your everyday life.

Your first access card to kingdom entrepreneurship is to realize that you only have one assignment. Your second access card to kingdom entrepreneurship is to recognize that you must always function in two arenas—the physical arena and the spiritual arena—at the same time. Your third access card to kingdom entrepreneurship is to remember that you are influenced by three atmospheres: the world-system, the kingdom of God on earth, and the kingdom of God in heaven. But you are required to avoid the world-system, take everything you need from the kingdom of God in heaven, and invest everything you've got in the kingdom of God here on earth.

Let's begin with your first access card. You have only one assignment. Genesis 1:27-28:

> **So God created humankind in his image, in the image of God he created them; male and female he created them. God blessed them, and God said to them, "Be fruitful and multiply, and fill the earth and subdue it; and have dominion over the fish of the sea and over the birds of the air and over every living thing that moves upon the earth."**

The one assignment that God gave to Adam and Eve is the same one assignment that you are still accountable to God to complete. The first part of the assignment requires you to be fruitful and multiply. Neither the first humans nor you had a problem with this part of your assignment. They liked sex, you like sex. Sex within a committed relationship causes reproduction. Non-committed sex whether in or out of wedlock causes sexually transmitted diseases including gonorrhea, syphilis, HIV and AIDS, to name a few. Non-committed reproduction activities cause you to multiply sickness, disease and death, while committed reproduction activities cause you to multiply health, wholeness and life.

Now the problem with Adam and Eve and you is that they and you stopped at sex and didn't move on to fill the earth with the knowledge of God and subdue it. And even today, you may be waiting for some political candidate to emerge who will control your neighborhood, your community, your state, your nation and your world, when you may be the leader you've been waiting for. God's mandate to you to rule the earth begins with your learning how to submit to His will so that you can rule yourself first. Only then will you be able to rule your own household. Then you can move out to rule your block, your neighborhood and on and on until you rule the nations according to God's ways and God's word. And just to confirm that you have only one assignment, Jesus repeated the assignment to His disciples right before He was taken up to heaven at Matthew 28:18-20:

> **And Jesus came and said to them, "All authority in heaven and on earth has been given to me. Go therefore and make disciples of all nations, baptizing them in the name of the Father and of the Son and of the Holy Spirit, and teaching them to obey everything that I have commanded you. And remember, I am with you always, to the end of the age."**

Jesus started out by making it clear to His disciples, His kingdom entrepreneurs, that He has all authority in heaven and on the earth. Based on this heavenly and earthly authority, He left you the same assignment as the Father gave you in Genesis: multiply disciples (kingdom entrepreneurs), replenish and fill the earth with kingdom entrepreneurs that you have made in every nation. Subdue the nations and have dominion over them by baptizing them and teaching them to obey the good news of the kingdom of God.

So your first access card to kingdom entrepreneurship is to realize that you have only one assignment. The Old Testament explains that assignment in natural, physical terms, while the New Testament explains the same assignment in supernatural, spiritual terms. It's the same assignment that has both a natural and a spiritual dimension.

Now, remember that for every kingdom access card there is a kingdom rule, a kingdom guideline and a kingdom leadership lesson. The kingdom rule that goes with your first access card of kingdom entrepreneurship is the rule of faith. You must believe the word of God to you that you must be about the one assignment that God has given you: to multiply, fill the earth, subdue it and have dominion over it both physically and spiritually. The kingdom guideline that goes with this first access card of kingdom entrepreneurship is the guideline of obedience.

Once you have faith and trust in God's word to you, then you must obey what He has said. Once faith has come, you can no longer make excuses for being disobedient to the word of God. So when you follow the rule of faith and yield to the guideline of obedience, then you can learn and apply the kingdom leadership lesson that goes along with faith and obedience. And that kingdom leadership lesson is that you must completely change the way you think from your way of thinking to God's way of thinking. In other words, it's your responsibility to transform your own thinking so that it is aligned with God's thinking. Proverbs 14:12 says: **There is a way that seems right to a person, but its end is the way to death.**

Your way of thinking may seem right to you, but it only leads you down the path to death. But God's way of thinking leads you to abundant life that death can't end no matter how hard it tries.

So, if you're using your first access card of kingdom entrepreneurship, then you're clear that you have only one assignment: to multiply, fill the earth, subdue it and have dominion over it both physically and spiritually. You have faith in and are obedient to the word of God, and you realize that you must transform and completely change the way you think to the way God thinks.

Now you're ready to deal with your second access card to kingdom entrepreneurship. Your second access card is to recognize that you must always function in two arenas simultaneously: the physical or natural arena that God commanded you to subdue and dominate back in Genesis, and the supernatural or spiritual arena that Jesus commanded you to subdue and dominate back in the Gospel of Matthew. So the issue becomes: how do you function in both the natural and the spiritual arenas at the same time?

The kingdom rule that goes with your second access card of kingdom entrepreneurship is the rule of wisdom. The kingdom guideline that goes with this access card is the guideline of sowing and reaping. And the kingdom leadership lesson that goes with this access card is that you must completely change and transform the way you behave to the way that God wants you to behave.

Let's start with the kingdom rule of wisdom. What is wisdom? Well, we know from scripture that the fear or reverence of God is the beginning of wisdom. But beyond the fear and reverence of God, what is wisdom? Dr. I.V. Hilliard says that wisdom is a disciplined approach to living in which you function from a spiritual perspective, and through discernment you apply both natural knowledge and spiritual knowledge to your personal situation, thereby bringing about the will of God in your life, which causes you to be truly wise.

In other words, because wisdom begins with the fear and reverence of God, it must manifest itself in your life by your living a disciplined, ordered, intentional and focused life in which you choose to function from a God mindset and not from your own mindset. When you function from a God mindset, you're able through the Holy Spirit to discern how to apply book knowledge and natural knowledge as well as Bible knowledge and spiritual knowledge into your situation.

In order to carry out your assignment to subdue the earth and make disciples (kingdom entrepreneurs) for the kingdom, you will need book knowledge and natural knowledge. You can't be without book knowledge and ignorant about what life is all about while trying to rule the world, nor can you rule the world without having good common sense. You need both, and living in wisdom will give you both. At the same time, you need to know what the word of God says and you need to have your own spiritual experience with God that backs up what you've read in His word. Bible knowledge will not save you or get you into the kingdom of God, but knowing Jesus personally will.

So you need to know the Scriptures and you need to know Jesus for yourself. Wisdom will give you both. When you practice this discipline of living in wisdom, you bring about the will of God in your life and you become wise in the process. As a wise person, you will depend on God for everything, be productive, accountable for your own thoughts and behavior, and always be a neighbor who seeks opportunities to help other people.

Now, the kingdom guideline that goes along with the rule of wisdom is the guideline of sowing and reaping. The bible says that what you sow or plant, you will reap or harvest. Whatever you plant will be what you harvest, except for the fact that what you harvest will always be much greater than what you planted. If you stop and help somebody who needs it; if you're accepting of those persons who are ostracized in your community and seek their welfare, then you will reap a harvest of love and favor from God and deep respect from the people you serve that is more than good measure, pressed down, shaken together and running over coming back strong to bless you.

On the other hand, if you refuse to help the poor and oppressed, and you act like HIV and AIDS, poverty and discrimination are not issues you need to address, then, you will reap a harvest of shame, disfavor from God, and disrespect from people who know you that is more than good measure, pressed down, shaken together and running over coming back even stronger to curse you.

The kingdom leadership lesson that goes along with your second access card to kingdom entrepreneurship is that you must completely change and transform the way you behave to the way that God wants you to behave. So, if you're living by your second access card of kingdom entrepreneurship, then you recognize that you must function in the natural and spiritual arenas simultaneously, that you must live under the rule of wisdom, respect the guideline of sowing and reaping, and completely change and transform the way you behave to the way God wants you to behave.

Your third access card to kingdom entrepreneurship is to remember that you are influenced by three atmospheres: the world-system, the kingdom of God on earth, and the kingdom of God in heaven. But you must avoid the world-system, take everything you need from the kingdom of God in heaven, and invest everything you've got in the kingdom of God right here on this earth. In order to rightly understand this access card, you need to start with the third atmosphere of the kingdom of God in heaven. Ephesians 1:3-6 will help you to do just that:

> **Blessed be the God and Father of our Lord Jesus Christ, who has blessed us in Christ with every spiritual blessing in the heavenly places, just as he chose us in Christ before the foundation of the world to be holy and blameless before him in love. He destined us for adoption as his children through Jesus Christ, according to the good pleasure of his will, to the praise of his glorious grace that he freely bestowed on us in the Beloved.**

What this passage is really saying is that when you follow Jesus by being a true kingdom entrepreneur, you have already been blessed by God with every single spiritual blessing that belongs to the Father and the Son in heaven. You don't have to die and go to heaven in order to benefit right now from the blessings that belong to you in heaven!

The writer goes on to say that the proof of your having been blessed with every spiritual blessing in the heavenly places is the fact that God chose you, picked you out, before he even made the world or set up its foundation. You are part of the first chosen people. God knew you and chose you millions of years ago before you were born into this world so that you would live a productive life before him by and through the love that God has for his Son Jesus.

This teaches you that you are not just how you were raised, or how you have been treated now or in the past, or even how you have lived up until today. But you have a history with God, the Father that goes way back before you were born. So you are not a slave to the world-system, your environment, or your past.

You were free when God called and chose you to be in Jesus eons ago, and you are free now when you take advantage of all the spiritual blessings that belong to you in heaven and apply them to your work on earth.

The kingdom rule of love, the kingdom guideline of service to others, and the kingdom leadership lesson that go with this access card to kingdom entrepreneurship show you how to access the kingdom of God in heaven.

The kingdom rule of love requires that you love God, your neighbor, and even your enemy as yourself. And lest you think that love is some syrupy sweet, warm, fuzzy feeling, let me remind you of Jesus' definition of love at John 14:23-24. Jesus defined love as being obedient to his word.

If you love Jesus you will do what he tells you to do in His word. If you don't love Jesus, you will not do what He tells you to do in His word. The promise that goes with loving and obeying Jesus is that He and the Father will come and make their home in you. When Jesus and the Father make their home in you because you love them, your neighbor and your enemy as you love yourself, then the kingdom of God on earth has come to you in order to influence the strategic way in which you think about, plan for and build your business by building the people around you who are helping you to succeed.

When you're not obeying God and not keeping the commandment to love given by Jesus, then you're being influenced and led by the world-system, which you've been warned to avoid. And the world-system is the enemy of the kingdom of God on earth and the kingdom of God in heaven. That's why the kingdom guideline of service to others is the means by which you can test your obedience to God and your keeping of the commandments of Jesus. When you serve the poor, the blind, the lame, the orphan, the widow, the HIV-infected and affected person, the junky and everyone else who is despised and rejected in your community, then the love of God and the keeping of Jesus' commandments are sown, grown, known and shown in you.

The leadership lesson that goes along with the rule of love and the guideline of service to others is that you must choose to completely change and transform your focus away from yourself to meeting the needs of hurting people. As you love God and obey the commandments of Jesus, the kingdom of God on earth lives in you and influences you to tap into all the spiritual blessings available to you in the kingdom of God in heaven. And through loving your neighbors and serving the needs of people, you are condemning, corrupting and overthrowing the world-system without shooting one bullet at anyone.

Under your first access card of kingdom entrepreneurship, you come to realize that you have only one assignment: to subdue the earth and have physical and spiritual dominion over it. You live by the rule of faith, you function under the guideline of obedience, and you choose to completely change and transform the way you think to the way God thinks.

Under your second access card of kingdom entrepreneurship, you come to recognize that you have to function in the natural and spiritual arenas simultaneously. You live by the rule of wisdom, you function under the guideline of sowing and reaping, and you choose to completely change and transform the way you behave to the way God wants you to behave.

Under your third access card of kingdom entrepreneurship, you are reminded that you are influenced by the world-system, the kingdom of God on earth, and the kingdom of God in heaven, but you must avoid the world-system, take everything you need from the kingdom of God in heaven, and invest everything you've got in the kingdom of God right here on earth. You live by the rule of love, you function under the guideline of service to others, and you choose to completely change and transform your focus from yourself to meeting the needs of hurting people.

When you use your three access cards of kingdom entrepreneurship, you guarantee for yourself that you will live out the natural, spiritual and transformational dimensions of being a kingdom entrepreneur: you will maximize the gifts, talents and resources God has given you; you will be a neighbor who refuses to pass by anyone in need; and you will transform the world by meeting the needs of its hurting people.

By living in wisdom this way, you will also guarantee for yourself that the words you hear from Jesus when He comes for you will be "Well done, you good and faithful kingdom entrepreneur." In the meantime, you will manifest the wealth and prosperity that your faith, action, hard work and tenacity have earned you—you will be rich right!

www.ingramcontent.com/pod-product-compliance
Lightning Source LLC
Chambersburg PA
CBHW070159230526
45471CB00002B/737